Drawing on a wonderful variety of theologians and researchers, Phil Maynard and Eddie Pipkin offer a thorough understanding of what it is to become a disciple like Jesus. They provide doable practices and exercises for growing disciples. Each chapter recognizes Disciple Challenges and offers what is Blessed. The authors also cite Additional Resources and provide solid questions for reflection with each chapter. Congregations seeking to become disciples like Jesus will grow by the study and use of this text.

Rev. Becky Balestri
Pastoral Leadership Revitalization Program Manager, Omaha Presbyterian Seminary Foundation

The reason any church exists is to make disciples of Jesus Christ as they help people experience God's grace through relationships and ministry. In *Disciple Like Jesus*, Maynard and Pipkin help the church reclaim that purpose. They do this by presenting the big picture of what it means to be a disciple as well as sharing the practical tools of how to develop a system for helping people move forward in their faith journeys. This resource provides the tools necessary to help the church be more healthy and vital as well as help individuals grow into the purpose that God has created them for as they move from knowing about faith to living their faith.

Rev. Kelly P. Brown
Director of Congregational Vitality, East Ohio Conference of the UMC

Step by step, concept by concept, and question by question, this book walks an individual or small group through a complete and structured understanding of what it means to be a disciple. This is an imminently practical and immediately useful book that can be understood and realistically put into action. Another great book by Dr. Phil Maynard and Eddie Pipkin!

Rev. Dr. Sarah Calvert
Arlington District Superintendent, Virginia Annual Conference of the UMC

Disciple Like Jesus is another excellent resource in a long line of excellent resources from Phil Maynard. If you long to go deeper in your faith, and lead others into an authentic journey following Jesus, *Disciple Like Jesus* will help you do just that. Filled with practical instruction and guiding questions, *Disciple Like Jesus* will help you take the next steps in your discipleship journey, and assist others to do the same.

Jeff Campbell
Associate General Secretary, Strategic Programming, Discipleship Ministries

What does it mean to live as a disciple of Jesus today? How can you become such a follower and effectively, faithfully lead others to this way of life? In *Disciple Like Jesus* Phil Maynard and Eddie Pipkin provide the framework, tools, and vision to shape and nurture authentic disciples. In Augustine's famous words, "Take up and read."

Rev. Dr. Gary S. Eller
President, Omaha Presbyterian Seminary Foundation

Maynard and Pipkin offer the Christian Church, its current and future leaders, and members an extraordinary, insightful, and practical guide for Christian discipleship for the 21st century church and beyond. All those who truly strive to fulfill Jesus Christ's commission and mission of becoming and making disciples for the transformation of the world by belonging, becoming, and blessing the world will benefit from the habits and practices shared by Maynard and Pipkin.

James L. Friday
Director of Congregational Development, South Carolina UMC Annual Conference

Disciple Like Jesus brilliantly unlocks the issue plaguing many churches today. Even with the church knowing their purpose is making disciples, most still struggle with discipleship. The church has confused discipleship as being about information and church membership. Maynard will help readers understand being a disciple is instead about personal transformation. Broken down into three main focus areas, this resource walks individuals through the discipling process of belonging, becoming, and blessing as we learn new behaviors as a becomer.

Kay Kotan
Church Growth Consultant & Co-author of *Mission Possible* and *Launching Leaders*

In Disciple Like Jesus, Phil and Eddie offer a rich and practical resource for leaders seeking to refocus on discipleship in their faith communities. In their focus on the life and teaching of Jesus, they present a clear framework for envisioning mature disciples which includes the spiritual needs of the disciple as well as the outward-oriented life of a disciple. The co-authors meet the current missional moment for the Church in the West by anchoring discipleship in intentional relationships and multiplication strategies rather than relying on programming, which makes *Disciple Like Jesus* helpful for those in traditional church contexts as well as those leading in distributed expressions of church. Phil's work has already been a blessing to The United Methodist Churches of Indiana, and I am confident this new resource will help us, and all who use it, to make maturing disciples of Jesus Christ.

R.C. Muhlbaier
Associate Director of Leadership Development – Laity & Discipleship, UM Churches of Indiana

If you only read one book on discipleship this year—this is the one to read! Phil Maynard and his writing partner, Eddie Pipkin, convey a clear understanding of how to initiate a contagious model of discipleship that replicates to others, much as the early Wesleyan movement did through one-to-one coaching and modeling along with transformation through accountability groups. Some books focus on theory and others on practice—*Disciple Like Jesus* offers both. Living the compelling message of the book helps us become more like Jesus and to enroll others in this lifestyle.

Dr. Larry Ousley
PCC & Retired Executive Director, Intentional Growth Center

How to Get the Most
from this Resource

Casting a Vision

For many congregations, there is a lack of clarity about what a disciple is and what a disciple does. Your congregation might find it helpful to have a larger conversation in worship or as a small group series around this theme. *Disciple Like Jesus* could provide the framework for this conversation. At the conclusion of each section, you will find a set of discussion questions that could support this conversation.

Small Group Study

There are many small groups of different varieties meeting at thousands of churches every week. They are forming bonds, supporting each other, often studying, and sometimes serving together. And yet, many people in many congregations sense there is something missing. They just don't know what that might be. *Disciple Like Jesus* could launch them on a new way of engaging life both within and outside of the Church.

Accountability Group

Each of the dimensions of discipleship described in this book includes specific suggestions for behaviors that help develop the "life of" ways of living like Jesus. Accountability is vital to this process. Whether through mentoring, apprenticing, coaching, small groups, or triads, partners can and should process this resource together. They should commit to specific behaviors, and hold each other accountable for progress.

Leadership Training

The greatest form of leadership in the Church is the leading of disciples toward maturity in becoming more like Jesus. There are skills, presented in *Disciple Like Jesus,* that can help develop more effective leadership toward this goal. In a strong sense, every disciple is called to be this kind of leader. But those publicly identified as leaders (in whatever role) have a biblically mandated special responsibility to be modeling this kind of discipleship development.

Personal Study

Disciple Like Jesus provides many tools for exploration for individuals into the ways in which they can become more like Jesus and disciple like Jesus did. There are also many references for further study and personal growth. We do believe, however, that while this is a great resource for individual study, it is even better to study with a friend or two.

Disciple Like Jesus

Making Disciples Like Jesus
Who Make Disciples Like Jesus

Phil Maynard

Eddie Pipkin

Market
Square
BOOKS

Disciple Like Jesus

Making Disciples Like Jesus Who Make Disciples Like Jesus

©2020 Phil Maynard & Eddie Pipkin

books@marketsquarebooks.com
P.O. Box 23664 Knoxville, Tennessee 37933

ISBN: 978-1-950899-13-5
Library of Congress: 2020936838

Printed and Bound in the United States of America
Cover Illustration & Book Design ©2020 Market Square Publishing, LLC

Publisher: Kevin Slimp
Editor: Kristin Lighter
Post-Process Editor: Ken Rochelle

Unless noted, Scripture quotations taken from the following version of the Holy Bible:

NIV

As noted, Scripture quotations taken from the following version of the Holy Bible:

MSG

Table of Contents

CHAPTER ONE

Defining Discipleship

A Tale of Two Neighbors

Marty doesn't consider himself religious. Sure, he believes in God, but it's been 25 years since he darkened the door of a church. He has a Bible, but he definitely doesn't read it every day, and he doesn't write checks to the church down the road (or any church, for that matter). He's retired, so his days are filled with puttering around the house. His special pride is his meticulously maintained landscaping.

His neighbor, Phil, on the other hand, is the definition of religious. He and his wife attend church regularly, sometimes more than once in the same week. They tithe their income, lead Bible studies, volunteer in the food pantry, and serve on a number of leadership committees.

On any given day, if you were to drive into the neighborhood, it is likely that you would see Marty sitting on the front porch of his home with several guys from the neighborhood, having a drink and catching up on life.

Phil, on the other hand, doesn't even know the names of those neighbors. He wouldn't recognize them if they bumped carts in the grocery store.

Marty always seems to be available to provide a helping hand. When Ann needed help getting her Christmas tree down from the attic, Marty went over and climbed up the rickety steps. When Steve couldn't get his car started, Marty showed up with the cables to give him a jump start. When Betty Jo needed an assist in rearranging some furniture, she called Marty. When Billy's deteriorating health meant he had to give up the car keys, Marty took him to appointments and shopping.

Phil, of course, never seems to be available. He's always busy at the church.

While Phil was away at the latest Christian conference and a snake got into his house, his wife called in a panic shouting, "There's a snake in the house!" Phil was a thousand miles away, so he said, "Call Marty." And Marty came over and caught the snake. Phil's wife texted him a picture of the snake-slaying hero!

So, who is the good neighbor in this story?

We share this parable (featuring true details with some name changes) because it illustrates two very important concepts about what it means to be a disciple of Jesus Christ.

First, if we were to take a vote to indicate which of the two parties (Marty or Phil) were the better disciple, most of you would identify Marty. That's because we identify intentional expressions of selfless love as reflections of Jesus, and Marty behaved in ways that the Gospels show us people who love Jesus should behave. This happened despite the absence of overt religiosity.

Phil, on the other hand, knew plenty about Jesus, but he had missed a lot of opportunities in his own neighborhood to actively reflect the life and love of Jesus. This was in spite of his household's overt religiosity.

Which clarifies the first critical point we want to make about discipleship:

Discipleship is not just about what you know. It's about what you do.

Or stated another way:

Discipleship is not just about information. It is about transformation.

Or stated still another way:

Discipleship is about behaviors.

This is a point worth exploring. In our work with congregations around the country, the most common perception about discipleship is that being a dedicated learner is equivalent to being an effective disciple. This is the clear result whenever we ask about a local congregation's process or pathway for discipleship. Inevitably, the pastor hands over a flyer that describes the different classes or "Discipleship Opportunities" that are available.

It is logical to define discipleship from the perspective of being "a learner." The word disciple itself comes to us directly from the Greek word, *mathetes,* which means student or learner.

What is not so commonly understood is that the meaning of the word (e.g. student, learner) has shifted over time. What it commonly means now is not the same as what it meant for people in biblical times, specifically within the context of the story of the life and ministry of Jesus. Lots of words have shifted meanings from then until now, as evidenced by these examples from Anne Curzon's TED Talk on the subject:

	In the past	**Now**
Cool:	low in temperature	on target or 'with it'
Nice:	silly, foolish	compliment
Silly:	worthy or blessed	weak, vulnerable, foolish
Awful:	worthy of awe	terrible things
Fathom:	circle with one's arms	understand after much thought
Clue:	a ball of yarn	evidence
Naughty:	having nothing	badly behaved
Bachelor:	young knight	unmarried man. [1]

In the same way, the understanding of a disciple being a student or learner is worlds apart from what it was in Jesus' day. Today, to be a disciple (learner or student) means to go to class or read a book, to study a subject extensively, or become an expert in a field. In the historical period in which Jesus lived, the discipleship process was more intimate and direct. Consider the following description from Dennis McCallum and Jessica Lowery in *Organic Discipleship:*

> Ancient Jewish discipleship was an educational process, but it contained much more than our modern concept of education. Rabbis transmitted knowledge, but the close association in daily life also transmitted elements not found in books. This

was personalized education where two men [sic] formed a close, trusting relationship in which the rabbi could sense and minister to inner spiritual needs in his disciple. He could see with his own eyes whether his trainees were living out what they had discussed. The idea was to produce a certain kind of person. The intensive personal attention involved in this style of training dictated that a rabbi focus on no more than a few disciples at a time.

Jesus took this model, used it, and expanding [sic] it. He lived and traveled with his twelve disciples and he seems to have focused even more on the top three: James, John, and Peter. Although some New Testament authors refer to all Christians as disciples (in the sense that they are all followers of Christ), by far the majority use of the word in the New Testament refers to those who were trainees of a specific teacher. [2]

The point of taking on a disciple was to form their lives to be like the rabbi. It was about formation, not just information.

Perhaps a better description than learner would be that a disciple is a becomer.

Wikipedia puts it like this:

In Christianity, disciple primarily refers to a dedicated follower of Jesus. This term is found in the New Testament only in the Gospels and Acts. In the ancient world a disciple is a follower or adherent of a teacher. It is not the same as being a student in the modern sense. A disciple in the ancient biblical world actively imitated both the life and teaching of the master. It was a deliberate apprenticeship which made the fully formed disciple a living copy of the master. [3]

Secondly, when it comes to discipleship, "we know it when we see it."

With Marty as our example, it's easy to identify the behaviors that we associate with the way Jesus lived. For example, Marty did these things:

- Made himself available to people.
- Met basic human needs.
- Enjoyed the companionship of a few close friends.
- Used his gifts to build up others.

It's perhaps more accurate to refer to our pal, Marty, as an "accidental disciple," because there is no sense of religious intentionality in the ways he replicates the generosity of Jesus, but the end result is clearly something to be admired by those of us who spend our lives intentionally seeking to be more like Christ. We have high opinions of those we observe who have achieved some measure of Christlikeness in their choices and habits.

Think of some of the people you personally know (or have known) whose lives actively reflect (or reflected) the life and values of Jesus. Take a few minutes, using the space below, and write down the names of those individuals.

_____   _____

_____   _____

_____   _____

Now, for each of the names you identified, write a brief description of why you identified this person as a powerful reflection of the life and values of Jesus.

Here's an example to get you started:

Bill	would give you the shirt off his back

Feel free to add more names and descriptions if needed.

Discipleship, even in the Old and New Testaments, was not limited exclusively to those who decided to follow Jesus:

- John the Baptist had disciples before Jesus did (Matthew 11:2, 14:12, Mark 2:18).
- The Pharisees had disciples (Matthew 22:16).
- Saul was a disciple of Gamaliel before he later became the Apostle Paul (Acts 22:3).
- There were disciples of Moses (John 9:28).

The modern confusion about what it means to be a disciple is exacerbated by scriptural accounts like the one found in the Gospel of John, chapter six. At the beginning of this chapter, the people shadowing Jesus from hillside to hillside were simply referred to as *crowds* or *people*. By the time we arrive at verse 60, apparently the very same people are called *disciples*. This is interesting, since Jesus had by then clarified that to be his disciple included taking him into oneself in dramatic meta-phorical terms ("eat my flesh and drink my blood"). To further amplify the confusion, Luke uses the same word, *mathetes,* translated as *disciple,* to describe those who explicitly believe in the Gospel message.

Jesus, however, makes it clear that there is a distinction between those just following him around for the chance to see a miracle or hear an inspirational sermon and those who were motivated to embrace the change he preached. The true followers of Jesus, the *becomers,* were unique in their focus on imitating Jesus. They were called to take Jesus into them. They were committed to becoming like Jesus as fully as possible.

Jesus did not hide the truth that those who committed to the "new life" he offered would be expected to change. Being a disciple meant more than just following him around from hillside to hillside like — to use a modern equivalent — Grateful Dead groupies.

The people closest to Jesus certainly did not take this call to radical change lightly. In John 6 we read these heartbreaking words:

> On hearing it, many of his disciples said, "This is a hard teaching. Who can accept it?" Aware that his disciples were grumbling about this, Jesus said to them, "Does this offend you? Then what if you see the Son of Man ascend to where he was before! The Spirit gives life; the flesh counts for nothing. The words I have spoken to you — they are full of the Spirit and life. Yet there are some of you who do not believe." . . . From this time many of his disciples turned back and no longer followed him (verses 60-66).

To be clear, the hard teaching wasn't hard in the sense that it was difficult to understand. The Greek word used is *skleros,* which means *rough, stiff,* or, figuratively speaking, something *harsh, unpleasant,* or *hard to accept.* It wasn't hard because it was incomprehensible. It was hard because it was intolerable. For many who liked much of what they were seeing and hearing, this call for complete, life-changing dedication was simply, as Eugene Peterson says, "too tough to swallow."

When we come across a statement like "this is a hard teaching," our immediate impulse is to investigate what the "hard teaching" is. So, let's go back to the beginning of chapter six. It becomes clear almost immediately that these people who are casually referred to as disciples are not truly disciples in the sense of becoming like Jesus. They are what might be considered pseudo-disciples for whom following Jesus meant just hanging around with him, perhaps exploring the possibility that he offers something special that can benefit them in some way.

Chapter six starts off with the feeding of the multitudes. So far, so good. Who doesn't want a Savior who will meet their needs?

Following that miracle, Jesus then walks on water. This is a little mind-blowing. It's a strong witness to Jesus' apparent superpowers. After all, if he can walk on water, is there really anything beyond his ability?

Up to this point, however, the focus is really all about them (those pseudo-disciples): what impresses them, what dazzles them, what miraculously meets their needs.

This is where we get to the hard teaching part. Jesus proclaims that if we want to be his disciples, then we are obliged to eat his flesh and drink his blood: "Whoever eats my flesh and drinks my blood remains in me, and I in them. Just as the living Father sent me and I live because of the Father, so the one who feeds on me will live because of me" (John 6:56-57). This is not a prophecy or prediction about what would eventually become the liturgical act of Holy Communion — that comes later. Here it is an incisive metaphor for the intentional act of *taking Jesus into us.* We choose to become disciples, and so choosing, we ingest all that Jesus is. Not only is something provided for us, but faithful partnership is expected of us. This should not be a surprise. Our relationship with God has always been a **covenant** relationship. God promises, "I will be your God." And God also says, "This is how you are to live." A covenant is a two-way pledge, and those who choose to follow God respond, "We will be your people" and "We will honor your ways." The Old Covenant (the Mosaic Covenant) was built on laws and sacrifices. The New Covenant (celebrated in our traditional liturgy of Word and Table) reflects the redemptive power of Jesus' sacrifice and resurrection for those who embrace the Good News.

It can still be a hard teaching, beautiful though it may be. The people who heard Jesus deliver the message "got it," but apparently a significant number of them were not interested in becoming like Jesus. They were content to just hang out with the crowds, marvel at his miracles, and celebrate their favorite aphorisms from his teaching and preaching. They were not excited about making sacrificial changes. They were not motivated to do life differently.

So, they no longer followed him around, or as *The Message* puts it, "They no longer wanted to be associated with him" (verse 66). Some sincere preachers and teachers, in wrestling with this text, soften the impact by saying that these pseudo-followers were just not ready to make that level of commitment and perhaps came around later. But the Greek word for *no* used in this passage is the strongest negative expression available, and it speaks unequivocally of complete and permanent change. Whichever way we look at it, the unwillingness of these people to take into themselves the mind, teachings, character, and behaviors of Jesus cut them off from the most amazing gift God has ever offered.

10

At the conclusion of the chapter in John, Jesus turns to his disciples (the ones who have actually been following him, learning from him, and becoming like him) and asks, "You do not want to leave too, do you?" Of course, it is Simon Peter who replies (isn't it always?), saying, "Lord, to whom shall we go? You have the words of eternal life. We have come to believe and to know that you are the Holy One of God" (verses 68 and 69).

Being a disciple was about more than shadowing Jesus like a gaggle of starry-eyed hangers-on. It meant these things:

- Going where Jesus went.
- Doing what Jesus did.
- Understanding the world from Jesus' perspective.
- Discovering the Kingdom of God at hand.
- Learning to think like Jesus.
- Loving the people that Jesus loved.
- Challenging the religious authorities.
- Carrying the message of Jesus to the ends of the earth.
- Turning the world upside down.

That calling to be like Jesus has not changed. It's no less a hard teaching than it ever was.

Consider the following extended excerpt from an article by Dan Dick, titled "Disciple Dissipation":

I listened with growing despair to a prominent United Methodist leader talking about our mission. Within just a few sentences he completely devalued and distorted the entire concept of discipleship:

"Once we say 'yes' to Jesus, we are forever after his disciples."

"Discipleship is a gift, a privilege — it comes at no cost."

"We (The United Methodist Church) have committed to get more disciples in worship each Sunday."

"We will have 648,626 new disciples worshiping weekly; 794,074 new disciples professing their faith; disciples growing through 443,952 small groups; 806,770 disciples serving God through mission in their communities, in their regions and all around the world; disciples giving $3.6 billion to missional ministries for God's mission in this world."

What definition of disciple is being used here? It certainly isn't a Christian disciple, and it obviously does not come from our Gospels. Our church is faced with two basic options:

1. To lift up a challenging and rigorous vision of discipleship grounded in our Scriptures that requires discipline, sacrifice, commitment, lifestyle change, values-based prioritization, and behaviors that reflect those of the Christ — and invite people to engage their faith at an entirely new level, or;

2. Reduce discipleship to a sham, debasing the Gospels and cheapening the example and teaching of Jesus the Christ so that discipleship is meaningless — something that anyone can claim with no investment or price.

So, hmmm, which one are we choosing?

We can pretend we are disciples all we want, but anything less than a radical reorientation is simply making a mockery of something holy and sacred. I close with the words of Wesley's covenant prayer — just something to reflect on when we try to decide what a disciple might actually look like . . . [and here he quotes directly John Wesley's covenant renewal prayer, a forceful affirmation and embrace of the cost of discipleship] . . .

I am no longer my own, but thine.
Put me to what thou wilt, rank me with whom thou wilt.
Put me to doing, put me to suffering.
Let me be employed by thee or laid aside for thee,
*   exalted for thee or brought low for thee.*
Let me be full, let me be empty.
Let me have all things, let me have nothing.
I freely and heartily yield all things
*   to thy pleasure and disposal.*
And now, O glorious and blessed God,
Father, Son, and Holy Spirit,
*   thou art mine, and I am thine. So be it.*
And the covenant which I have made on earth,
*   let it be ratified in heaven. Amen.*[4]

Dick joins the clarion call of leaders from a variety of traditions and denominations for the Church to rediscover a commitment to making disciples of Jesus, not just followers of Jesus or students of Jesus or learners about Jesus or, as Kyle Idleman famously wrote, fans of Jesus. Our world is in desperate need of a Church of becomers, witnessing to the possibilities of the Kingdom of God ushered in by Jesus.

The late Dallas Willard, a professor at the University of Southern California, author, and a leading thinker in the area of discipleship, agreed:

For at least several decades the churches of the Western World have not made discipleship a condition of being a Christian. One is not required to be, or to intend to be, a disciple in order to become a Christian, and one may remain a Christian without any signs of progress toward or in discipleship.

Contemporary American churches do not require following Christ in his example, spirit, and teaching as a condition of membership — either of entering into or continuing in fellowship of a denomination or local church. . . . So far as the visible Christian institutions are concerned, discipleship clearly is optional.[5]

This attitude, lamented by Willard, is at odds with the teaching of Scripture and the message of the Gospels. Confronting it, however, raises a 'sticky' issue in the Church. On the one hand, the Scriptures say we are "saved by faith," not by works. On the other hand, "faith without works is dead." The theologian N.T. Wright summarizes:

Christians, particularly in the Western world, have for a long time been divided between 'epistles people' and 'Gospels people.' The 'epistles people' have thought of Christianity primarily in terms of Jesus's death and resurrection 'saving us from our sins." The 'Gospels people' have thought primarily in terms of following Jesus in feeding the hungry, helping the poor, and so on.

This either/or split does no justice, in fact, to either the epistles or the Gospels. Still less does it do justice to Jesus himself. For him, the Kingdom which he inaugurated could be firmly established only through his death and resurrection.[6]

It is the death and resurrection of Jesus that frees us from the power of sin to begin living into the Kingdom life. Wright suggests language to describe this behavioral transformation:

Jesus is in fact inviting his hearers to something . . . we might call eschatological authenticity. Yes, there will be a time when God's people will serve him, love him, and live out the genuine humanness of which the ancient Law had spoken "naturally" and from the heart. But this will be a God-given "second nature," a new way of being human. ***And you can begin to practice this now*** . . . because Jesus is here, inaugurating God's Kingdom.[7]

Eschatological is a fancy theological term that refers to the end times. What Wright is saying is that in God's long-term plan, all who follow Christ will be perfected as a corollary of Christ's second coming, but that process begins now. It's a simultaneously mystical and practical process, and Christians have long debated the mechanism by which it is accomplished. There are those who focus on the working of the Holy Spirit to effect the transformation, trusting that whatever God wants them to be and do, God will accomplish supernaturally within them. On the flip side are those who suggest that this transformation occurs through the relentless pursuit of relevant behavioral changes, so that we arrive gradually but inevitably at a destination of righteousness.

Again, this is not an either/or situation. Christ's death and resurrection broke the stranglehold of sin. The power of the Holy Spirit pours the fullness of God's unmerited love into our lives (God's grace). And so, we choose to become like Jesus, engaging in behaviors that lead us toward that eschatological authenticity Wright describes.

John Wesley, the Anglican priest/theologian and founder of the Methodist movement and author of the prayer of covenant renewal we referenced earlier, looked around 1740s English Christianity and saw stagnation and complacency. He called for transformative revival, and this transformation's catalyst would be an outpouring of God's grace, given an outlet of expression through a commitment to habits of personal and social holiness. His most recognized expression of this life-altering transformation was this question:

Are you going on to perfection?

He did not mean, of course, absolute perfection (for, obviously, only God is perfect). It is the wholeness, or completeness, the *teleios,* the goal of genuine humanness, for which he quests. This is the same word that Jesus used in Matthew's version of the story of the rich young ruler (Matthew 19:21) where Jesus said, in effect, if you want to be 'complete,' then go and sell your possessions, give to the poor, and come and follow me. This was not about the young ruler following a series of commands, conforming to a list of rules, or pledging fealty to a detailed set of behaviors, but rather developing a character formed by overflowing, generous love.

So, there are two significant themes at play in the process of discipleship, two principal ways of becoming, two paths of moving toward completeness/wholeness/perfection. First is the working of the Holy Spirit pouring the grace into our lives which keeps us longing for this wholeness and the power to overcome the bondage of sin that would keep us less than whole. Second is the commitment to engage in the intentional process of becoming, a process empowered by active learning, application, and accountability.

Again, Wright notes the significance of these two factors in the development of maturing disciples:

> This is the whole point of saying, as wise Christian theologians always have, that the way grace works is by the Holy Spirit enabling us to become, at last, truly human. [8]

> What does all this tell us about Christian virtue? Simply this: that the life to which Jesus called his followers was the Kingdom life — more specifically, the Kingdom-in-advance life — the life which summoned people to be Kingdom agents through the Kingdom means. The habits and practices of

16

heart and life to which they were called were the habits and practices which demonstrated in advance that God's Kingdom was indeed turning the world the right way up, cleansing the world so that it would become the dwelling place of God's glory.[9]

With a goal of becoming like Jesus and an enthusiasm for being open to what the Holy Spirit wants to accomplish in our lives, in the next chapter we'll consider the question that motivates all who would move from an intellectual exercise to practical application:

But what does that look like?

Questions for Reflection and Discussion

1. What has been the most significant factor in your growth and development as a disciple of Jesus Christ? How has that changed the way you do life?

2. What might it be like to have discipleship in our culture reflect the rabbinic practice of intensive personal attention described in the quote from *Organic Discipleship?*

3. Identify five people from your congregation that you believe reflect maturity as a disciple in some dimension of their life. For each person identified, describe the behavior/way of living that brought them to mind.

4. What was the 'hard teaching' described in John 6? Is it still a hard teaching today to consider that something is expected of us as disciples?

5. Dallas Willard is quoted as saying, "One is not required to be, or to intend to be, a disciple in order to become a Christian." What is your experience in making a commitment to Jesus? Were there clear expectations for discipleship?

CHAPTER TWO

What Discipleship Looks Like

So, what does a disciple becoming like Jesus do? How are they called to live their lives? What distinguishes them from other followers of famous leaders like these:

- Martin Luther King, Jr.?

- Mahatma Gandhi?

- Mother Teresa?

Over the years, a variety of leaders in the Church have identified attitudes, habits, and disciplines that set the disciples of Jesus apart from the followers who professed allegiance to other inspirational leaders. One thing that there seems to be agreement on is this: once we undertake the process of personal transformation toward a Jesus-like life, the evidence of our progress is measured by our ability to change specific behaviors. Alan Hirsch, a missionary from Australia to the United States and author of several books, puts it this way:

> I simply do not believe that we can continue to try to think our way into a new way of acting, but rather, we need to act our way into a new way of thinking. [1]

Dallas Willard makes the same point in a slightly different manner:

I can tell you that the transformation of character comes through learning how to act in concert with Jesus Christ. Character is formed through action, and it is transformed through action, including carefully planned and grace-sustained disciplines. [2]

This is consistent with what brain scientists are learning through research into our neural pathways, as recounted by Tara Swift in *Forbes Magazine:*

For the brain to rewire itself it requires sustained practice of a new behavior which will sufficiently challenge the brain to think in a new way. Imagine how difficult it is to learn a new language or take up a new instrument — this is how hard your brain needs to work to stimulate growth and forge new neural pathways. [3]

In the previous chapter you identified people who reflected the life of Jesus, and you specified some of the notable behaviors that caught your attention. When we do this exercise with discipleship teams in local congregations, they generate a surprisingly consistent list of such behaviors. People who consistently reflect the life of Jesus. . .

- Seem to have a direct connection to God through prayer and other spiritual practices.
- Are always helping someone in need.
- Really know the Scriptures.
- Are willing to give sacrificially to help someone in need.
- Build strong relationships with people outside the church.
- Share their faith.
- Are passionate in personal and corporate worship.

- Partner with less mature believers to help them grow.

- Support the ministries of the church.

- Get involved in mission trips.

- Tithe and even go beyond the tithe to address special needs.

In Phil's previous work as a Congregational Developer in the Florida Conference of The United Methodist Church, he and his team discovered that local churches often had trouble expressing a clear understanding of what it meant to be a disciple of Jesus. This was surprising, because it seems like a basic concept that underpins the whole purpose for a local church's existence. It would be the equivalent of showing up at a gym where the owners can't tell you the definitions of *fitness* or *exercise*. To get to the bottom of this conundrum, the congregational development team brought together a group of about thirty key laypeople and clergy, divided them into pairs or triads, and asked them to put together a list of identifying characteristics for disciples of Jesus. How do disciples do life (in ways that differentiate them from non-disciples)?

This group identified about 150 things that disciples do. They quickly concluded that you couldn't bombard a newly professing believer with a list of 150 things for which they were immediately accountable! But as they analyzed those lists of characteristics together, they also realized they had a clear consensus on some core behaviors that personified Jesus' first principles. (We'll share those consensus behaviors with you in a bit.)

George Barna, in his book *Maximum Faith,* searches for direct evidence from the Scriptures to identify a similar set of behaviors:

- Lovers of God
- Passionate worshipers of God
- Repentant sinners
- Joyful
- Forgiveness
- Acceptance
- Invitation/evangelism
- Lovers of people
- Humble
- Friends
- Abundant faith
- Students of Scripture
- Prayer warriors
- Lovers of truth
- Fasting
- Obedient
- Holy
- Fearless believers
- Role models
- Integrity
- Morally blameless
- Persecuted believers
- Trustworthy servants
- Seekers of justice
- Merciful
- Supporting the needy
- Grateful receivers of God's gifts
- Generous stewards [4]

John Wesley, who developed the accountability systems of discipleship that became the Methodist movement, formed groups he called Holy Clubs, and he later expanded them to include variations called Class Meetings and Bands, each of which was built on the foundation of covenant relationships. The Class Meetings — not classrooms in the contemporary sense, but organized gatherings with designated leaders and clear structures — were focused on the practice of modeling specific Jesus-like behaviors. The Bands were focused less on enforcing accountability for specific behaviors and more on exploring attitudes, emotions, feelings, intentions, and mental states associated with those behaviors. The motivation for these highly organized discipleship systems was a desire to grow in what Wesley termed "living holiness" and "purity of intention." Consider the following expression of the Class Meeting Covenant (shared here using the modern language employed by the Accountable Discipleship ministry used by some Methodist congregations):

- I will pray each day, privately, with my family and friends, and for my covenant members.
- I will read and study the Scriptures each day according to a plan.
- I will worship each Sunday unless prevented and receive the sacrament of communion.
- I will heed the warnings of the Holy Spirit not to sin against God or my neighbor.
- I will heed the promptings of the Holy Spirit to serve God and my neighbor.
- I will prayerfully seek to care for my family and home and seek to help someone in need each day.

- I will prayerfully care for my body and for the world in which I live.

- I will prayerfully plan the stewardship of my resources.

- I will share in Christian fellowship each week where I will be accountable for my discipleship. [5]

Now, take a look at how these specified behaviors (committed to by the meeting members in the Class Meeting covenant) morph into more expansive, all-consuming concepts — spiritual ways of being — for the early Methodists who had advanced to Band Meetings. Band Meetings were the accountability groups for more mature disciples. Here are the questions they asked one another, complete with the original 1770s phrasings:

1. Have you the forgiveness of your sins?

2. Have you peace with God, through our Lord Jesus Christ?

3. Have you the witness of God's Spirit with your spirit, that you are a child of God?

4. Is the love of God shed abroad in your heart?

5. Has no sin, inward or outward, dominion over you?

6. Do you desire to be told of your faults?

7. Do you desire to be told of all your faults, and that plain and home?

8. Do you desire that every one of us should tell you, from time to time, whatsoever is in his heart concerning you?

9. Consider! Do you desire we should tell you whatsoever we think, whatsoever we fear, whatsoever we hear, concerning you?

10. Do you desire that, in doing this, we should come as close as possible, that we should cut to the quick, and search your heart to the bottom?

11. Is it your desire and design to be on this, and all other occasions, entirely open, so as to speak everything that is in your heart without exception, without disguise, and without reserve? [6]

To bring it back into contemporary terms, James White, pastor at Mecklenburg Community Church, in his book, *Rethinking the Church,* identifies the five key traits of disciples through use of the acronym, TRAIN:

- **T**eaching: Knowledgeable about the Bible, theology, and doctrine.

- **R**elationships: Life change happens best in the context of deep relationships.

- **A**ttributes: Developing the fruit of the Spirit.

- **I**nvestments: Commitment to spiritual practices and disciplines.

- **N**eeds: Someone who has a heart for the needs of others. [7]

You may have begun to notice a pattern. Based on our study of dozens of systems of discipleship and our interaction with a wide range of congregations utilizing these systems in real world applications, we have summarized these behaviors with the following definition:

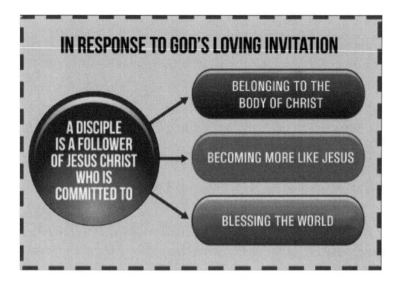

For those seeking a biblical basis for this definition, look no further than Matthew 4:19, where Jesus offers this quixotic invitation:

"Come, follow me" = **Belonging to the Body of Christ.**

"And I will make you" = **Becoming more like Jesus.**

"Fishers of men" = **Blessing the world.**

These are three broad categories of behaviors (or ways of being). Jesus doesn't get into the nitty-gritty details of the 'what' or 'how' within these categories, and that's intentional. That comes later. This Matthew 4:19 invitation — which, after all, marks the very beginning of the apostles' mind-boggling journey — sketches the basic outline of the three major pillars of the life of an authentic disciple. Picturing these three discipleship pillars as the supports of a three-legged stool might be helpful. Each leg is equally important. The foundation is sturdy and stable only if each leg is equally strong.

Whenever we teach this material in workshops, we also take a moment to remind everybody that a disciple is a follower of Jesus Christ *for life.* Retirement is not the end goal of the discipleship career path. We keep on keeping on, always honing our discipleship skills. This is possible because of the creative flexibility incorporated within the discipleship process as modeled by Jesus. There is no one rigid accreditation standard . . . do these ten things in exactly this way, and you get your discipleship merit badge! We are free to explore our individualized path to discipleship. For each of the three categories represented in the three-legged stool illustration (each of three separate but interrelated ways of being), there are many different routes one can take to fulfill one's unique future within that category (belonging to the body of Christ, becoming more like Jesus, and blessing the world).

In the category of *belonging to the body of Christ,* disciples discover deep relational connections with God and with one another. These relationships foster support, encouragement, challenge, accountability, and inspiration. Ultimately, we answer our call to grow the body by connecting with all the people beyond the walls of the church, as we are equipped to invite others to discover God's love for themselves.

In the category of *becoming more like Jesus,* disciples engage in the spiritual practices modeled by the Messiah that keep us in connection to God's grace, help form our lives to the will of God, and provide opportunities for us to help others grow in their discipleship.

In *blessing the world,* disciples discover the joy of giving of themselves and their resources to meet the needs of others. They use their gifts, talents, time, and financial assets to serve and make a Kingdom difference, addressing both mercy and justice issues, just as Jesus did.

We will focus together on a menu of specific behaviors and practices that can help us live into these unique ways of being. However, the goal of discipleship is not just to check these practices off a to-do list, but to allow them to transition us to new ways of thinking and living. Changed behaviors lead to transformed lives. But the goal is not the accomplishment of the changes themselves. George Barna makes this distinction clear:

> [T]he term transformation is not synonymous with the word change. The two terms differ in scope and significance. . . . Change is a refinement that is typically short-term, impermanent, incremental, superficial, and of limited ultimate consequence. In contrast, transformation is generally long-term, permanent, systemic, deep, and monumental in its impact and consequences. Change merely alters a known

reality; transformation radically redefines that reality. . . . God wants you to be transformed.[8]

What belonging to the body of Christ, becoming more like Jesus, and blessing the world will look like in the life of any individual disciple will overlap with what those ways of being look like for other disciples, but they may also be distinctly different. There is no set curriculum or cookie-cutter approach. There is no one-size-fits-all box into which we are required to squeeze.

For example, one disciple may find that the spiritual practice of contemplation is the most helpful way for them to experience that deep connection with God and God's grace, while another may find that an intensive study of Scripture is the most helpful. Both will engage the Word, but in ways that meet God's calling on their lives. Phil worked with a wonderful disciple who found God speaking in his life through intensive study of the Scriptures (what they call exegesis in seminary).

This kind of study profoundly affected this disciple's view of the world. However, as studious as he was, he could never wrap his head around Phil's love for the technique of using guided meditations to reflect on select Scripture passages. They both found the Word to be a source of inspiration and guidance. God just wired them with different ways to get there.

One disciple may find a calling to serve the working poor in their own neighborhood, while another may be called to go to Africa and provide wells for communities in need of clean water. Both are discovering the joy of giving of themselves and their resources to meet the needs of others. A guy we know named Joe has had a successful career in developing and running a coaching business serving non-profit service organizations around the southeastern U.S. He has been blessed with amazing success, and he recently started volunteering as a mentor for local high school students.

He recently said, "I feel like this is God's new calling for my life. It is such a blessing to help these young people see possibilities for their lives." Sarah, on the other hand, just returned from a trip to Mozambique where she provided prayer support for an on-site mission team. Both have discovered the joy of giving themselves to others. Both ways are valid and honor God.

Despite their differences in application, what these examples demonstrate is how committed disciples move from concepts to action. We internalize what we learn, and then we work out our unique calling to put principles into practice. To get us closer to the practical behaviors which are expressed within each of the ways of being a disciple (belonging to the body of Christ, becoming more like Jesus, and blessing the world), we have found it helpful to break out some "lifestyle" categories within each dimension of discipleship.

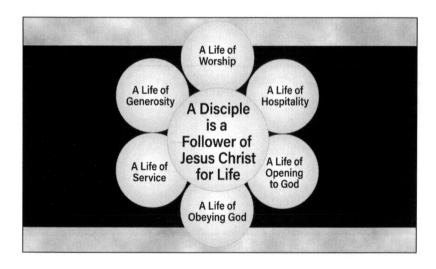

Belonging to the Body of Christ through a Life of Worship

Disciples are designed to worship God. As author Louis Giglio puts it:

> You are and always will be a worshiper.
> It's what you do.
> You can't help it.
> You can't stop.
> You can't live without it.
> But you can choose where you invest it . . .
> We're created to worship. [9]

Notice the language. This includes participating in worship together, an activity that has been a focus of the people of God for thousands of years and through which we are drawn into a deep experience of the presence of God and offer ourselves into that relationship. As the people of God gather to offer a chorus of praise and thanksgiving, they witness to the amazing grace of their own lives and the life of their chosen faith community, and they join in celebration of all that God has been and will be doing in their midst. But a life of worship is bigger than attendance at corporate worship.

It is about a daily lifestyle in which we are drawn into God's presence through our personal devotions. It's about cultivating an awareness of God's presence in the way all of life is lived. We see this in the stories of faith heroes like Brother Lawrence, as recounted in *The Practice of the Presence of God:*

> We find him worshiping more in his kitchen than in his cathedral; he could pray, with another:

Lord of all pots and pans and things . . .

Make me a saint by getting meals

And washing up the plates!

And he could say, "The time of business does not with me differ from the time of prayer, and in the noise and clatter of my kitchen, while several persons are at the same time calling for different things, I possess God in as great tranquility as if I were upon my knees at the blessed sacrament." [10]

A life of worship means we make our relationship with God a priority by spending time devoted to building that relationship through praise, prayer, meditation, and reflection on the Scriptures and life. But it also includes honoring God in the ways we live our daily lives. To worship is to bring honor and glory to God.

This includes a breadth of opportunities, including how we choose to use the resources God has provided to us, how we care for creation, how we engage other people and see them in the image of God, and how we do our jobs, offering our best as though serving God directly rather than just earning a paycheck.

Jesus modeled a life of worship:

- John 4:23-24 (when he prophesies that a time is coming in which "true worshipers will worship the Father in spirit and in truth").

- Matthew 4:10 (when he chastises the devil with the rejoinder that one should "worship only God").

- Matthew 26:26-27 (when he leads the disciples in the Last Supper by instructing them, "Take and eat; this is my body" and "drink [from this cup]").

But his worship life was not merely centered around organized gatherings with readily recognizable aspects of what we would consider formal worship. Everything about his life was designed to bring honor and glory to God, from his disdain for materialism and the trappings of fame and power, to his teaching, to his miracles, to his concern for society's outcasts:

- He welcomed the refugees and the rejects with the hospitality of God.
- He went off by himself to spend time alone with God.
- He went to the temple and gathered his disciples in times of the religious feasts in Jerusalem.
- He celebrated the offerings of tears and expensive perfumes, as well as the widow's mite.

We, too, are called to his model of offering our lives in worship in these ways.

Belonging to the Body of Christ through a Life of Hospitality

Disciples have experienced the amazing hospitality of God first-hand. Through the grace of Jesus Christ, we have been loved, accepted, and welcomed into the Body of Christ. We, in turn, are called to offer that same hospitality to this world that God has loved so much that God gave his Son that it might be redeemed. Hospitality is an expression of God's love through us. This is bigger than shaking a hand or offering a seat in worship. Hospitality is making room in our lives for 'the other.' It doesn't matter whether 'the other' is a fellow member of the Body of Christ, a neighbor, a stranger from the community, or a traveler from a distant land.

The other person doesn't have to be like us or meet some arti-
ficial standard we have set. They don't have to be from the same
ethnic, racial, socio-economic, or lifestyle group as we. Henri
Nouwen, Roman Catholic priest and author, puts it this way
when he describes the ministry of presence:

> It is a privilege to have the time to practice this simple
> ministry of presence. Still, it is not as simple as it seems . . . I
> wonder more and more if the first thing shouldn't be to know
> people by name, to eat and drink with them, to listen to their
> stories and tell your own, and to let them know . . . that you do
> not simply like them — but truly love them. [11]

Jesus modeled a life of hospitality. No one was outside the
circle of his loving acceptance and care. He welcomed tax collectors, sinners, the woman at the well, and the woman who had
been caught in the act of adultery. He calls us to follow his lead
with compassion and empathy:

- He calls us to invite the poor, crippled, lame, and the blind
  (Luke 14:13).
- He calls us to show hospitality to strangers (Matthew 25:35).
- He calls us to give a cup of cold water to the thirsty
  (Mark 9:41).
- He calls us to welcome the children (Luke 18:15-17).

We, too, are to look for opportunities to extend God's gracious
welcome to all.

Becoming More Like Jesus through a Life of Opening to God

Any relationship is grown and enhanced as we spend time

together and focus on one another. Disciples recognize that their relationship with God follows the same pattern. Disciples engage in spiritual practices that provide a deep connection to God and place themselves in the flow of God's grace into their lives. That grace is a free, unmerited gift of God's love, and disciples seek to be open to that flow of grace as they make that relationship a priority. We use the following image to help describe this process of engagement.

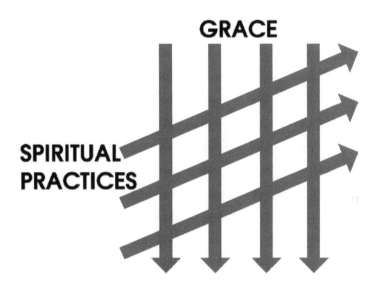

Jesus modeled this life of opening to God as he did these things:

- Engaged in solitude
- Prayed
- Encouraged fasting
- Quoted Scripture
- Worshiped

We, as disciples, are called to the spiritual practices that open us to God's love through the working of the Holy Spirit.

Becoming More Like Jesus through a Life of Obeying God

The Scriptures tell us that to Jesus "all authority has been given . . . on heaven and on earth" (Matthew 28:18). Disciples of Jesus discover that obeying God brings abundant life. When we do what he tells us to do, our lives are lived in the will of God, just as Jesus the Son's life was lived in the will of God the Father.

This dimension of obedience builds on the life of opening to God as a disciple moves from the experience of God's grace in their own life to the sharing of God's grace with others through changing their behaviors to align with God's teaching. The more they discover of God's truth, the more change results. As a disciple embraces this Jesus-oriented life, they discover that they are transformed and thus become agents of transformation in the wider world.

Jesus modeled this life of obedience to God:

- Drawing on Scripture to make decisions (for example, in his confrontation with Satan).
- Welcoming the sinner.
- Discipling others.
- Seeking God/God's will through prayer.
- Giving his life on the cross.

Eugene Peterson describes the way this attitude of obedience takes shape within us:

[W]e are formed by the Holy Spirit in accordance with the text of Holy Scriptures. God does not put us in charge of forming our personal spiritualities. We grow in accordance with the revealed Word implanted in us by the Spirit. [12]

Disciples of Jesus do the things Jesus says to do. They replicate the attitudes and actions that Jesus modeled. They even become disciplers of others in his name (people who intentionally guide other people in the process of discipleship).

Blessing the World through a Life of Service

Disciples live out the joy of serving others. They find that blessing others through their words and deeds brings a sense of blessing to their own lives. Just as Jesus modeled a life of service, his followers support the needy by feeding the hungry, healing the sick, clothing the naked, ministering to those who are prisoners (both the incarcerated and those imprisoned by their own economic circumstances, toxic relationships, and mental issues) — all of which we call mercy ministries. They also engage the powers of society to seek justice for the oppressed, outcast, impaired, and those unable to fend for themselves — which we call social justice ministries.

Jesus modeled a life of service every time he did these things:

- Healed the sick (Matthew 8:1-3, in which he healed a leper).
- Fed the hungry (Matthew 14:13-21, in which he fed the 5,000).
- Attacked the systems that abused the poor (John 2:13-22, in which he cleared the temple courts).

Disciples of Jesus, likewise, develop a lifestyle of serving others. John Wesley, theologian and founder of the Methodist Movement, puts it this way:

Do all the good you can.
By all the means you can.
In all the ways you can.
In all the places you can.
At all the times you can.
To all the people you can.
As long as ever you can. [13]

Blessing the World through a Life of Generosity

Disciples of Jesus discover the blessings of using their resources, time, energy, and skills to have an impact in the world. They live within financial margins (spending less than they earn), so that they can respond to needs that God puts in their path. They support the Kingdom work by their tithes and offerings, so that the church might have the resources to transform the world. Disciples recognize that everything they have and all the resources with which they have been blessed are gifts from God, who trusts them to use those resources wisely.

We don't own them; God does. They are merely "on loan" to us, as stewards, to be managed faithfully, ethically, and responsibly.

Jesus modeled a life of generosity:

- He pointed to the sacrifice of the widow's mite (Luke 21:1-4).

- He called us to give to God what is God's (Mark 12:17).

- He willingly gave up his own life on the cross for our redemption (John 15:13 and John 3:16).

Disciples of Jesus develop a lifestyle of generosity. Again, John Wesley, in a sermon called "The Use of Money," has coined a pithy set of phrases that boil the principles of godly generosity down to their essentials:

- Earn all you can.

- Save all you can.

- Give all you can. [14]

While we have identified some behaviors modeled by Jesus, as well as important principles that Jesus taught, the goal is not just to simulate those behaviors or parrot those teachings like some apostolic automaton. The goal is to have those behaviors and principles become so engrained in our decision-making process that our whole way of living moves closer to God's holy standards.

In theological terms, we call this process sanctification. The Holy Spirit works in and through us so that we may become more Jesus-like in every aspect of who we are and what we do.

Religious thinkers for two millennia have suggested ways to describe this process of ongoing transformation. John Wesley uses the language of "going on to perfection." Jesus uses the language of going on to completion (*teleios*). The Bible uses a variety of images to communicate this movement:

- Undertaking a journey (3 John 6-7).

- Coming home (Zephaniah 3:20).

- Putting on the armor of light (Romans 13:12).

- Putting on the armor of God (Ephesians 6:11-12).

- Running the race (Hebrews 12:1).

In the next chapters, we will begin to explore in more detail the many varieties of spiritual practices and behaviors that can fuel our growth in belonging to the body of Christ, becoming more like Jesus, and blessing the world. You will observe that for each of the dimensions of growth we have discussed, common to each dimension is a recurrent theme of movement towards transformation. This is the act of *becoming* that is the natural state of the disciple. The defining characteristic of this revolutionary movement from our old selves towards God's ideal is that we are focused less and less on ourselves — our needs, our desires, our struggles — and more and more on the needs, desires, and struggles of others.

Discipleship is not about us and what we get from the deal. It is about how we are becoming like the One who, in every dimension of his being, was continually focused on others, sacrificing himself in every way in every moment to the service of others.

Questions for Reflection and Discussion

1. We quote a couple of thought leaders in the arena of Christian discipleship, pointing out that the development of our character, our journey toward Christlikeness, and our transformational ways of thinking happen through the interplay of grace and action in our lives (intentional spiritual disciplines, empowered and sustained by grace). What spiritual practices have helped you think about the world differently? Give specific examples.

2. The image of a three-legged stool is used to describe the three broad dimensions of discipleship (belonging, becoming, and blessing). Which of those legs (dimensions) feels strongest for you? Which might require some development to reach maturity?

3. George Barna describes a clear distinction between change and transformation. Which best describes your journey as a disciple? Why?

4. Brother Lawrence, in *The Practice of the Presence of God,* suggests that it is possible to be fully in God's presence even while doing the mundane things of life. In what ways have you experienced this?

5. Spiritual practices (disciplines) are described as a way of placing ourselves in the pathway of God's grace. How do you understand grace to be at work in your own life? What practices do you engage in to intentionally place yourself in grace's pathway?

CHAPTER THREE

Belonging to the Body of Christ

Belonging to the Body of Christ Through a Life of Worship

One cannot view the life of Jesus without recognizing that *everything* he did brought honor and glory to God. From announcing the inbreaking of the Kingdom of God to healing the sick and raising the dead, to teaching expansive new perspectives on forgiveness and love, everything he said and did was designed to glorify the Father. It was all an affirmation of ways to worship God.

Jesus was baptized, taught in the synagogue, and celebrated the traditional religious feasts. He went off by himself to spend time alone with the Father. And, of course, he practiced what he preached as he engaged the everyday challenges of life.

This is what a life of worship looks like.

The following graphic comes from a diagnostic tool we developed at Excellence in Ministry Coaching called the Real Discipleship Survey. This survey begins with the premise that our discipleship journey of "going on towards perfection" proceeds through stages from exploring our faith, to taking beginner's steps, to steady growth, to eventual maturity. We can see where we are along this continuum toward maturity because there are specific behaviors that correlate with each stage of growth. If we are honest about what behaviors we are practicing, then we have a good sense of our current status. Here's an example for considering the life of worship.

A LIFE OF WORSHIP			
I attend worship when a friend invites me, when it is convenient, or when I feel a need.	I attend worship regularly, but I am growing to realize that I must attend to God every day.	I attend worship regularly and set aside time daily for personal worship.	I honor God in the ways that I work, play, and engage others in relationships.

You can see the clear progression of attitudes and resulting behaviors. It's a movement from thinking about worship as a singular, structured event to thinking about worship as a holistic lifestyle.

Worship is about bringing honor and glory to God through the way we live. The Apostle Paul helps us understand this kind of all-in lifestyle, as he writes in Romans 12:1-2:

> So here's what I want you to do, God helping you: Take your everyday ordinary life — your sleeping, eating, going-to-work, and walking around life — and place it before God as an offering *(The Message)*.

This, of course is the end-goal. Most of us start out by attending an organized worship service led by a professional clergyperson in a designated sanctuary in a local church building (which is the familiar activity that we refer to as corporate worship). There is great merit in participating in corporate worship. Worship services provide valuable opportunities:

- **To Connect:** Corporate worship brings the body of Christ back together, a re-membering of the body — to support, encourage, and challenge us.

- **To Celebrate:** We are encouraged in our faith and the possibilities for our world as we celebrate the ways we have seen God at work in our midst.

- **To Communicate:** Corporate worship both teaches and models the vision of God's Kingdom and encourages our next steps in the journey of discipleship.

- **To Commit:** Worship is a way that we are placed in the path of God's grace and prompted to take the next steps in our journey.

- **To Consecrate:** Worship both reminds us of and provides an opportunity for us to be a people that are 'set apart' by our discipleship.

Here's a story from Phil that witnesses to the power of corporate worship.

It was Saturday evening in the middle of an amazing spiritual retreat weekend. The community had gathered for worship out in the country in a white-framed church that was at least a century old. In this space, where generations of believers had sung praises, prayed prayers, and shared the Word of God together, the Spirit was palpable. We joined the communion of the saints in worship as we lifted our voices in praise and prayer, reflected on the Scriptures together, shared our stories, recommitted our lives, and celebrated at the table of the Feast.

In preparation for the arrival of participants for worship, we lit our candles in the darkened space and sang praise to God who had been at work in dramatic ways. As we, with glowing faces, processed down the aisles between pews, there was not a dry eye in the room. We were there to celebrate what God had been doing. We were there to witness to our faith. We were there to encourage the faith of others.

As we left that holy space, each of us understood that our lives had been altered in some unmistakable way. We were no longer on our own. We had become part of something bigger than ourselves. We had metamorphosed into passionate participants in the mission of God.[1]

There had really been nothing unique about the details of this worship service. They had been, on the surface, much the same as most worship services in which Phil had participated. But then something special and memorable had somehow broken through. In fact, it was so powerful that in over twenty-five years of ministry, Phil has had a passion — a longing if you will — to be part of making this same kind of impact on people's lives. Could every weekly worship service impart that same break-through sense of God's people deeply and profoundly connecting with the Spirit?

He wrote down his insights about what had set this worship experience apart, and he's used this list of touchstones as a guide in designing worship experiences in the two decades since:

- It isn't about us. The worship experience is about God and focusing our praise and thanksgiving toward the source of our being.

- It isn't showy. The experience can and should be carefully planned and well-conducted, but we need to be careful to be open to what the Spirit wants to do.

- It is focused. The preaching/teaching of the Word is practical and focuses on putting into practice what God wants for our lives.

- It is experiential. The participants in worship are engaged in acts of worship rather than as spectators in a worship event.

- It is relational. We find a joy in gathering with other believers having a similar focus in life, and we are encouraged as we encourage others.

However, even corporate worship that gets all those things right can feel empty to us if we don't do our part to be full and eager partners in the process. The goal is not to 'go' to worship but to offer ourselves in worship, to be open to what God wants to do in our lives, and to receive instruction about possible next steps in our journey:

- Do we enter worship with a sense of expectation (that God is going to meet us there)? Do we look forward to an opportunity to offer public praise? Do we hope to be challenged? Have we prepared our hearts by reading the Scripture and the sermon preview?

- How do we engage with the message presented in worship? Do we make notes — either in our Bible or in a journal? How do we listen for God's invitation to take the next step? Do we continue to reflect on the Scripture/message beyond the worship experience? With whom do we process what we are learning from God's Word?

- As we experience the worship service, what do we notice about the way people are welcomed and cared for? Given hope? Prayed for? Encouraged? How could we build on these insights in our lives?

- As we provide our tithes and offerings, do we feel a sense of joy about giving our resources to make a difference in this world? Are we encouraged to give also of our time and energies to support the Kingdom work?

The Psalmist gives us a beautiful vision for worship with impact:

> Blessed is the person . . .
> whose delight is in the law of the Lord,
> and who meditates on his law day and night.
>
> That person is like a tree planted by streams of water,
> which yields its fruit in season
> and whose leaf does not wither —
> whatever they do prospers.
>
> **Psalm 1, verses 1-3**

While it is important to gather in corporate worship (because things happen in corporate worship that are hard for an individual to replicate), it is equally essential to have a personal time of worship, which is commonly referred to as a devotional time. This personal worship is the catalyst for our constant delight in the Lord, day and night. It is a wellspring of spiritual sustenance. And just as a corporate worship experience has underlying core values, an effective personal devotional time features important ingredients:

- **Place:** Having a designated place that is "God's space" is helpful. Some prefer the beach. Some have a room set up as a chapel for their special time with God.

- **Praise:** Singing or listening to hymns or praise songs or reading the Psalms of praise are all great ways to celebrate God's goodness.

- **Prayer:** Prayer is our line of communication with God where we share our needs, affirm God's provision, and pay attention to God's guidance.

- **Plan:** It is helpful to have a plan for devotional reading and the study of God's Word for our lives.

- **Presence:** Enjoy your time with God! Clear your mind of other concerns and be fully present in the moment.

- **Progress:** Journaling what God is revealing to you and tracking your prayer life can be a great way to focus and track your progress on your faith journey.

There are two main goals of this time of personal worship/ devotional time. First, just like with corporate worship, there is great value in offering ourselves specifically in actions of worship. Second, this time of paying attention to God is also a time that begins to form our awareness of God's invitation to engage life's normal activities as an opportunity for worship. A favorite author, Ken Gire, in a book titled *The Reflective Life*, suggests three habits to support this process:

- **Reading the Moment:** reading the Scriptures, reading the newspaper, paying attention to what is going on around us.

- **Reflecting on the Moment:** using our mind to engage what is going on beneath the surface (lessons from the Word, perspectives and world views being communicated).

- **Responding to the Moment:** giving what we have seen a place in our heart . . . allowing it to grow . . . upward to God and outward to other people. [1]

This kind of thoughtful analysis leads directly to the development of an awareness of the presence of Christ throughout the day and our response to this presence. There are many exercises for developing this awareness and responding to it faithfully. You might consider an ancient spiritual exercise called an The Daily Examen (or Examination of Consciousness). It is generally undertaken as a conscious, prayerful review at the conclusion of the day of all that day's activities (imagine reviewing a recording of your day) and developing an awareness or consciousness of how God was present or pushed away at each given moment.

Worship, public and private, prepares us to live a worshipful life. It helps us be thoughtful and faithful as we answer these existential questions:

- How do I choose to use my time? Am I thoughtful about the way my hours are spent, or do I waste time frivolously that might have been used to a higher purpose?

- How do I choose to use the resources God has provided? Do I keep the needs of others in mind, or am I completely focused on fulfilling my own needs and desires?

- How do I focus on loving my spouse and family? Do I make the important relationships in my life a priority, or do I squeeze them in haphazardly?

- How will I interact with a difficult person? Do I have forgiveness and understanding in my heart, or am I always looking for payback or avoiding those who vex me?

- What is the priority I place on spending time with God? Is time set aside for my Creator part of my regular routine, or is God just someone I call on when I need something?

- What is my level of faithfulness in following through on commitments? Do I take my obligations seriously, or am I an expert at justifications and excuses?

- What is my commitment to excellence when performing the tasks of my job? Do I treat assignments in ways that honor God with my integrity and work ethic?

These are imminently practical decisions that are made as we move through each day. They don't get resolved during a one-hour worship service on Sunday. They are made moment by moment in the real world, and each decision we make is direct evidence (for good or ill) of how we're following through on our commitment to live as a follower of Jesus. The truth is every choice we make can be an opportunity to worship God or not.

For example, let's say you have a small windfall and now have some extra cash. You can either use it to purchase the Apple Watch you've been secretly coveting, or you can provide additional support to an orphanage in Honduras that your friend has been telling you about. The decision you make is either an opportunity to worship God or a decision to feed your own material desires.

Or, let's say you're walking down the street and, uh-oh, here comes Joe. Everybody knows Joe's a talker. Let him get a word in edgewise, and it'll be twenty minutes minimum. You're on your way to a meeting. Stop to acknowledge Joe, and there's no way you'll make it on time. What to do? Your decision reflects an opportunity to worship God or not.

A life of worship is lived with an awareness and celebration of the presence of God in all moments at all times.

That awareness is the product of intentional development in the life of a disciple. It may begin with the corporate worship experience, but its continued development requires time and commitment to expand the relationship. You may have heard the phrase, "It's like they have a direct line to God." There are people who seem to dramatically exemplify that phrase. This doesn't take place by accident or happenstance. It is a connection with God that is developed through building a relationship and practicing an awareness.

51

Once every couple of months or so, while Phil is sitting in his home office, he'll become aware of the sounds of praise songs coming from outside. In a loud, confident tenor, the insect control technician for the home next door is lifting his voice in praise to God while he ensures a pest-free environment for God's people. It's not a showy thing. He just can't help himself. His life is about bringing glory to God.

This 'bug man' also happens to be a member of the church where Phil worships. The 'bug man' recently shared a testimony during worship where he described God leading him to provide free pest control services to a family caring for a physically challenged child. When asked why he had done this, he gave a simple response: "Because my boss [pointing skyward] told me to." Bonus to the story: showing up to help at that place at that time led to a chain reaction of three new customer accounts. As the 'bug man' put it, "You really can't out give God."

As we participate in public and private worship, immersing ourselves in the Scriptures and opening ourselves to what the Spirit is revealing to us about God's will for our lives, we grow in our insight into how we can bring glory and honor to God in all situations. As we pray for our families, our neighbors, our communities, and our world, we begin to develop the heart of God for the people God loves.

Jesus modeled both public and private worship. We fixate on the massive crowds that followed him from hillside to hillside, but sometimes we forget how he also modeled the importance of getting away from those crowds to be alone with God the Father, using this time apart to recharge and refocus on the mission. With all the distractions of his day and the ongoing pressure of all the needs of the people he encountered, Jesus understood the importance of keeping the connection with the Father/Creator strong. So, we find him in the early morning engaged in a time of solitude, praying to the Father. At the beginning of his ministry, when Jesus is faced with the temptations in the desert, we find him drawing on the truths of Scripture to define his life (and perhaps we notice that he had the relevant verses memorized). Later, faced with the dark shadow of the death of a friend, he raises Lazarus by crying out directly to the Creator of life. That's a strong bond.

The God-honoring life is powered by the depth of the relationship built by spending time with God and deepening the connection, day by day, working through each challenging circumstance as it presents itself. Growing toward maturity in this dimension of discipleship begins to form everything we do so that each action, from the mundane to the momentous, becomes a moment that can bring glory and honor to God:

- Skipping a night out with the girls to be there for a friend in need.

- Choosing to volunteer at a community ministry/service organization over binge-watching your favorite TV series.

- Using all or part of your vacation time to go on a mission trip to South America.

- Not yelling at the referee when you're righteously certain they've made a poor call.

- Getting home in time for dinner with your family instead of finishing the project at work.

- Sharing your faith story with a friend or colleague.

- Valuing the co-worker in the office as a person reflecting the image of God.

- Doing your job with integrity when a difficult choice is required.

- Standing up for someone who is being oppressed or bullied.
- Refusing to laugh along at an inappropriate joke.

The life of worship is just that — life — a normal life, lived extraordinarily. Growing toward maturity in this dimension of discipleship begins to form everything we do, every choice we make, every word we say:

- Are we seeing Christ in other people?
- Are we doing everything we undertake with excellence, as though serving God directly?
- Are we attuned to the warnings and promptings of the Holy Spirit and responding to those warnings and promptings?
- Are we meeting the needs of others who cross our path, even if meeting their needs means sacrificing some of our desires and preferences?

For the next three chapters, as we consider the specifics of belonging to the body of Christ, becoming more like Jesus, and blessing the world, we'll include some bonus material at the end of each section. These additional "Disciple Challenges," resources, and recaps, in addition to the discussion questions, are designed to help you focus on important takeaways and develop plans for converting concepts to action plans.

Disciple Challenges

Remember that what we are aiming for here is to develop a lifestyle of bringing honor and glory to God — a life of worship. While this lifestyle is not limited to any specific behavior or grouping of behaviors, it is our behaviors that form the ways that we think and engage our world:

- Participate in corporate worship regularly. Journal about what you learn and how you are inspired and challenged to grow as a disciple.

- Set aside a few minutes each day specifically to spend time with God. You may find it helpful to read a verse or two of Scripture and pray about what God is speaking into your life.

- Meet with a friend or two each week and respond to this question: Where have I seen God at work in my life this past week?

Blessed . . .

The call to be worshipers cannot be ignored. It is who we are, and we will always be engaged in worship. To worship the Creator of all things is only natural, and God delights in God's creation celebrating God's goodness. When we engage in a lifestyle of worship, we experience a growing awareness and delight in the presence of God in all of life.

We begin to see God's hand in providing for the created. We become aware of guidance and power to be who we are called to be. We get to love God even more!

Resources you might find helpful

- *Foundations: An Introduction to Spiritual Practices,* by Phil Maynard (available at the Excellence in Ministry Coaching website at emc3coaching.com, as well as marketsquarebooks.com and cokesbury.com)
- *Celebration of Discipline,* by Richard Foster
- *Sacred Rhythms,* by Ruth Haley Barton
- *Discipler: An Interactive Guide to Intentional, Relational, and Accountable Discipleship,* by Phil Maynard and Eddie Pipkin

Recap for a Life of Worship

A life of worship is about a growing awareness and delight in the presence of God in all the moments of our daily lives and about engaging with God in such a way that we seek to grow in that presence, bringing honor and glory to God through our words and deeds.

Supporting Scripture verse:

> **"Love the Lord your God with all your heart and with all your soul and with all your strength and with all your mind."**
>
> **Luke 10:27**

Behaviors that reflect a life of worship:

- Spending intentional time with God to develop the relationship.
- Gathering with other disciples to celebrate how God has been experienced in our midst.
- Developing an awareness of how our decisions, actions, thoughts, and deeds can bring honor and glory to God.

Questions for Reflection and Discussion

1. Why do you think coming together for worship might be an important part of our faith development?

2. Describe a worship experience where you were prompted to take a clear step forward in your journey as a disciple.

3. Describe briefly the most meaningful worship experience in which you have participated. What made it so special?

4. What is your experience of having a daily devotional time/ personal worship time? What practices do you engage?

5. Describe a decision you have made that you believe brought honor and glory to God.

6. This section of this chapter identifies four things that reflect a life of worship (seeing Christ in the other person, doing everything with excellence, responding to warnings and promptings of the Holy Spirit, meeting a need in your path). Describe a personal experience with one of these ways of offering worship.

7. What will you commit to this week to grow in your life of worship?

Belonging to the Body of Christ
Through a Life of Hospitality

A central theme witnessed throughout the life of Jesus is the offering of God's hospitality to all the people that God loves so much that God sent the Son to bring them into the Kingdom life. The list of people to whom Jesus directly offered this grace-filled hospitality was expansive (to the point of controversy):

Pharisees	Sadducees	Sinners
The wealthy	Prostitutes	The poor
Sinners	Lepers	Tax collectors
The Demon-possessed	Samaritans	Gentiles
Fishermen	The lame	The blind

This new kind of hospitality was actively practiced by Jesus, and he encouraged all who followed him to extend the same kind of hospitality. This fresh take on an old practice was defined by vastly widening the circle of those considered worthy of respect and compassion:

- **Individual Welcome and Acceptance:** All persons were welcome to be a follower of Jesus, no matter their pedigree or history: persons from all walks of life, diverse socio-economic status, different ethnic and cultural backgrounds, varying lifestyles, physical and mental status, religious practices, and of course, sinners of all variety.

- **Development of Authentic Community:** From traveling with the twelve disciples to eating at the table with sinners, Jesus encouraged the development of deep relationships. He offered God's forgiveness and spoke truth to those who were distorting the nature of God's Kingdom for their own gain. He challenged established perspectives and opened the people's understanding of the inclusiveness of the Scriptures. Most of all, Jesus modeled doing life together. He understood the value of sharing experiences and supporting one another on the journey to spiritual maturity.

- **Witness to the World:** Beyond the intimate community Jesus built with the twelve disciples, he advocated for the hospitality of God to be extended to all people. These people weren't required to fulfill any advance requirements to justify the hospitality extended to them; they didn't have to meet any standard of lifestyle, ethnic/cultural identity, code of religious conduct, degree of health, or even mental stability. Jesus offered acceptance, healing, forgiveness, companionship, and redemption to unexpected people in unexpected places, all as a witness to God's love.

- **Invitation to Kingdom Life:** Whether during structured teaching times, chance encounters along the road, intentional confrontations with religious leaders, private moments with seekers, or everyday conversations with his disciples, Jesus invited people to the new reality of the Kingdom life. He routinely used phrases like "the Kingdom of heaven is at hand," "go and sin no more," and "you have heard . . . but I say to you." Everything about his words and actions invited people to a new way of understanding their world and a new way of engaging life.

This is what it means to live a life of hospitality.

The following graphic (reprinted from the Real Discipleship Survey) shows a progression of behaviors that reflect growth toward maturity for a disciple committed to living out Jesus' vision for this life of hospitality.

A LIFE OF HOSPITALITY

I am curiously drawn to the Christians who graciously accept me as if I belong with them already.	I am called not only to receive, but also to offer God's gracious acceptance to others.	I seek to relate to others both in the church and beyond in ways that reflect God's hospitality to me.	I intentionally seek to build relationships with unchurched people in order to share God's love.

Hospitality is about how we welcome, accept, and engage other people. It's about how we invite them to Kingdom living. This includes people we are close to, people who are neighbors, and people who are casual acquaintances. It even includes people who are complete strangers. Henri Nouwen, priest and renowned spiritual guide, puts it this way:

> Hospitality is about making room for other people
> in our lives. [2]

While hospitality in our contemporary culture is most often defined as a form of "fellowship" where we get together with friends, the biblical tradition saw hospitality differently. In Bible times, hospitality was a serious cultural obligation that was focused on welcoming the stranger. In the Old Testament, we see many stories in which hospitality is extended to accommodate those with physical needs for shelter and nourishment, but Jesus extends the concept further, gathering in those who knew the profound pain of exclusion and isolation. Those who turned to him found acceptance and the promise of being included in the Kingdom of God. Not only did he urge his followers to generously welcome those in need, but he promised that these acts of kindness were also an offering of love to the Son of Man, himself, as related in Matthew 25:40: "The King will reply, 'Truly I tell you, whatever you did for one of the least of these brothers and sisters of mine, you did for me.'"

It's not just about us!

If we are living the life of worship we talked about in the previous section, this life of hospitality is a natural expression of our discipleship. We love because we have been loved. We welcome others because we have been welcomed. We invite others to discover this grace because we, ourselves, have experienced the transforming power of God's grace. This multi-faceted relational interplay is the dynamic that drives our witness in the community, our worship as the body of Christ, and our growth in maturity as disciples.

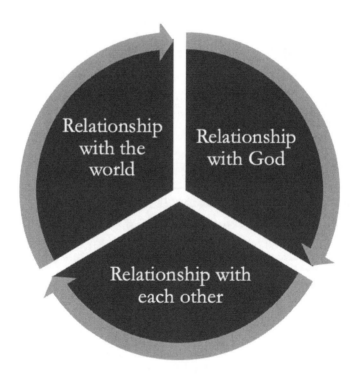

Each aspect of relationship feeds the others and ultimately makes us part of a process that draws other people to an experience of Christian community and a relationship with God through Jesus Christ. It was this very kind of witness that launched the Christian movement in the first century. Michael Frost describes it this way:

> These ordinary believers devoted themselves to sacrificial acts of kindness. They loved their enemies and forgave their persecutors. They cared for the poor and fed the hungry. In the brutality of life under Roman rule, they were the most stunningly different people anyone had ever seen. Indeed, their influence was so surprising that the fourth-century emperor Julian (AD 331-363) feared that they might take over the empire. [3]

A life of hospitality begins with being attracted to an experience of community where people engage one another differently.

To really benefit from the hospitality expressed by the community of faith, we must develop a sense of authentic connection. This requires more than putting our name on a membership roll. This sense of belonging and engagement comes from the development of deep relationships within that community. It means getting involved. It means interacting with others in ways that allow them to know us and be known in return. Janice Price of the Church of England World Mission Panel writes:

> Hospitality, as the mutual indwelling one with another, becomes the modus operandi of mission as those in common participation in the life and mission of God meet and receive from each other.... Hospitality is an attitude of the heart

which is about openness to the other. . . . This mirrors the hospitality of the Trinity as God chooses to open himself to the other through the Incarnation and to subject himself to the created order. . . . It is about a generous acknowledgement and meeting of common humanity as well as meeting the needs of humanity, emotional, spiritual, and physical, with generosity. As such it mirrors the activity of God towards creation. [4]

The route by which these deep connections happen is, of course, a two-way street. On the one hand, the church offers a wide variety of opportunities for people to get together at large events, in small group ministries, and through focused programs for people with common interests (youth, children, seniors, men, women, singles, recovering addicts, etc.). Churches also offer work teams, spiritual studies, fellowship hours, and even fitness classes. But potential participants must be willing to extend themselves to give these options a try. Connections can't happen if people sit home on their hands.

Often, participation in relational opportunities results in people finding someone with whom they really connect, and lifelong friendships are formed. The Gallup Organization, in *Growing an Engaged Church,* reports that this depth of relationship is one of the key factors in people staying involved and becoming more engaged in the life and ministry of a given congregation.[5] And while these congregational connections are essential to healthy local congregations, we will fall short of the life Jesus calls us to if we are not engaging people beyond the walls of the church. This engagement can take a variety of forms, as witnessed by the life of Jesus. For some people what is needed most is just a friend with whom to share life. For others it may be providing a listening ear as they go through a personal crisis or a helping hand to deal with a practical problem.

Disciples discover the great joy of being there for someone, or as John quotes Jesus at the Last Supper:

> **"Greater love has no one than this; to lay down one's life for one's friends."**

John 15:13

Barring an opportunity to "lay down one's life" in dramatic, cinematic fashion, disciples are called to lay down their lives bit by bit, moment by moment, foregoing their own desires to love and serve others. This lifestyle of hospitality is called Incarnational Ministry by missionary and author, Alan Hirsch. It's empowered by the concepts of presence and proximity.

Hirsch describes **presence** as our Christian witness through our commitment to deep relationships:

> If relationship is the key means in the transfer of the Gospel, then it simply means we are going to have to be directly present to the people in our circle. Our very lives are our messages, and we cannot take ourselves out of the equation. . . . But one of the profound implications of our presence as representatives of Jesus is that Jesus actually likes to hang out with the people we hang out with. They get the implied message that God actually likes them.[6]

For Hirsch, presence is complemented by the idea of proximity. Proximity is about being involved in people's lives in ways that impact those lives and witness to God's love and concern for them:

> Jesus mixes with people from every level of society. He ate with Pharisees as well as tax collectors and prostitutes. If

we are to follow in his footsteps, his people will need to be directly and actively involved in the lives of the people we are seeking to reach. This assumes not only presence but genuine availability, which will involve spontaneity as well as regularity in the friendships and communities we inhabit. [7]

Disciples of Jesus should practice both presence and proximity. All this verbiage sounds complicated, but following Jesus' example to act in hospitality can be surprisingly straightforward. One of the key ways we launch into this level of hospitality is the simple act of eating together. If you want to get to know people better, take them to lunch, dinner, breakfast, coffee, or ice cream. The table, even from the days of ancient Israel, has always functioned as a place of hospitality, inclusivity, generosity, and grace. At the table we share stories. We share hopes. We share dreams. And we confide our fears, disappointments, or disillusionment. We've even been known to get real about our faith in Jesus.

Just recently, Phil and his wife, Becky, invited a new person at their church to join them for lunch. (This would be a truly bold move for most of us long time churchgoers!) They spent about an hour and a half together with the new fellow and basically got his entire life story. It turned out that he really needed someone to talk to, and he really appreciated the opportunity to connect.

Alan Hirsch and Lance Ford, in *Right Here, Right Now,* celebrate the power of sharing food together:

Sharing meals together on a regular basis is one of the most sacred practices we can engage in as believers. Missional hospitality is a tremendous opportunity to extend the Kingdom of God. We can literally eat our way into the Kingdom of God! If every household regularly invited a stranger or a poor person into their home for a meal once a week, we would literally change the world by eating![8]

Whether it's through the breaking of bread or some other get-together — whatever we choose from the unlimited menu of options for connecting with other people — the ultimate outcome of Jesus-style hospitality is that through our lives people are invited to discover the fullness of God's love for themselves and make their own commitment to become disciples of Jesus. In other words, when we live fully into this life of hospitality, we help others become disciples.

Some of you are developing an allergic rash right about now . . . worrying we're about to launch into a pitch for classic one-on-one evangelism. It's intimidating for many disciples to think about this process in traditional evangelical terms, which can sometimes begin with a confrontational script to "get right with God," skipping over the part where God's love offered through our hospitality has created a safe space for conversation to occur. If we lead with hospitality instead of an agenda, the progression is natural and makes sense (without the awkwardness of forced evangelism).

Here's an example that illustrates this kind of natural progression. About twenty-five years ago, Phil and Becky discovered a Tex-Mex restaurant in Fort Lauderdale while attending a convention just down the road. It looked like a hole-in-the-wall kind of place from the outside (which is, of course, an attraction to Phil and many foodies). It turned out to have some of the best Tex-Mex food that he had ever tasted, and Phil travels a lot! The salsa was incredibly fresh, and the owners made hand-pressed corn tortillas which, with a little butter, made the perfect appetizer. The Tacos al Carbon were amazing. To top it off, this restaurant's version of fried ice cream, was sweet, gustatory perfection — and fun, too!

It was such an enjoyable experience that they make it a point to go back whenever they're in the area, and "in the area" means anywhere within a couple of hours' drive time. It's that good. In fact, so good that they began to enthusiastically tell their family and friends about it. They even started taking some of these lucky people along with them on their tortilla road trips. Over the years, they've probably been responsible for half a hundred new customers discovering this one restaurant.

It's just natural to share something that has impacted our lives for the better. When we read a good book, we tell a friend who might enjoy it. When we see a good movie, we can't stop talking about it. When we discover a great place to eat, a cool new activity, an interesting exhibit, or a great new song, we broadcast the good news. We want people to experience the same joy we have experienced, to grow in the way we have grown. Our experience with Jesus is no different. Our enthusiasm for our local church home is contagious. We naturally want to invite others to be a part of the unique Jesus-centered community that helps bring meaning to our lives.

This is not a new phenomenon. In fact, we see it demonstrated repeatedly in the Scriptures. One of our favorite examples is found early in the Gospel of John:

> **The next day Jesus decided to leave for Galilee. Finding Philip, he said to him, "Follow me." Philip, like Andrew and Peter, was from the town of Bethsaida. Philip found Nathanael and told him, "We have found the one Moses wrote about in the Law, and about whom the prophets also wrote — Jesus of Nazareth, the son of Joseph." "Nazareth! Can anything good come from there?" Nathanael asked. "Come and see," said Philip. When Jesus saw Nathanael**

approaching, he said of him, "Here truly is an Israelite in whom there is no deceit." "How do you know me?" Nathanael asked. Jesus answered, "I saw you while you were still under the fig tree before Philip called you." Then Nathanael declared, "Rabbi, you are the Son of God; you are the king of Israel." Jesus said, "You believe because I told you I saw you under the fig tree. You will see greater things than that." He then added, "Very truly I tell you, you will see 'heaven open, and the angels of God ascending and descending on' the Son of Man."

John 1:43-59

People still come to know Jesus primarily through a relationship with a disciple of Jesus.

To suggest the flow such introductions should follow, congregational excellence expert Jim Ozier includes this graphic in his book, *Clipped In.*[9]

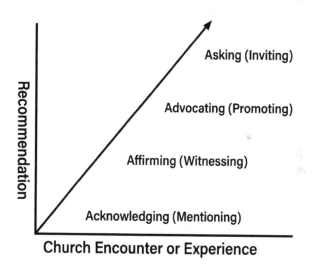

Inviting People to Church

Asking (Inviting)

Advocating (Promoting)

Affirming (Witnessing)

Acknowledging (Mentioning)

Recommendation

Church Encounter or Experience

You've first established a relationship with another person (neighbor, co-worker, or new friend), and the flow begins with a mention that you are a Christian and hang out with other Christians. Maybe you are later asked a direct question about faith. Maybe your friend mentions her sick mother. At any rate, there is a logical segue for you to bring up your faith life. This gives you an opening in the following weeks to share a little about your own journey, and if your friend still seems interested, you can talk about your specific experience with your own faith community. If your friend shows continued curiosity, it makes all the sense in the world to issue a personal invitation to join you at an event or small group gathering. That's flow.

Of course, you can't get in the flow, if you're lacking in the know. The hospitality flow is dependent on our connection to other disciples, our connection to a worship and accountability community, and our connection to other people in the big, wide world.

First, if you are not in partnership with someone who is a disciple, perhaps someone from your church, we encourage you to take advantage of one or more of the many options offered by most local congregations to make relational connections. There is nothing that will make it feel more like you belong than making a friend. Look for ways to be involved in serving at the church. Churches are always looking for volunteers to support a variety of ministries. This is also an amazing way to meet people and develop friendships. When you go to church and sit next to someone you don't know or don't know well, take a moment and introduce yourself and invite them to share some of their story. Don't always sit in the same place for worship. Move around and maximize the potential for meeting someone new. If you're the someone that the someone who is new to your church meets, take an opportunity to do a deeper dive and invite them to lunch following worship or arrange to meet for coffee the following week. They will be blessed, your church will be blessed, and you will be blessed.

We need to develop hospitality skills within a supportive, nurturing environment to ready us for the reality that Jesus said to "go and make disciples." Literally, this verse reads, "Therefore, wherever you go, make disciples." It's not enough for us to "move on towards perfection" in our personal lives. Jesus set an expectation that disciples will make disciples. This is not something best accomplished through some big evangelistic campaign. Rather, it is something we do through living by Christ's principles and connecting with others, person to person.

Wherever we are, Jesus is inviting us to be a witness to our becoming more like him. This is an invitational type of life. People are drawn to those who live a Kingdom life. We are invited to see every moment as an opportunity to witness to the difference this life can make. Specifically, we are instructed to be intentional about seeking opportunities to share our faith; to be prepared to share our faith when asked; to pray for those who do not yet have the same life-giving relationship with the Creator we have discovered; and to be intentional about building the kind of relationships where we might have the opportunity to be an expression of God's love.

Of course, if we take the charge to "go and make disciples" seriously, not only will we extend the hospitality that leads to relationships, but when that moment comes when a person asks about our faith experience, we'll have a clear plan for what it is we want to say. Too many disciples stumble over these opportunities, but it doesn't have to be that way. Be thoughtful about the words you'll use and the stories you'll tell (before it's time to share). You can practice this skill just like you'd practice any skill. There are techniques to help think it through. For instance, an Acts 22 approach uses the Apostle Paul's testimony as a guide. He uses a three-part structure to share his story:

- What his life was like before he knew Christ (Acts 22:1-6).

- How he came to know Christ (Acts 22:6-16).

- What his life was like after he came to know Christ (Acts 22:17-21).

It's a straightforward model. Write your story down. Practice sharing it with an accountability partner or in a small group. Another useful tool is an exercise called a Symbol Timeline. You can find an example at the www.emc3coaching.com/ resources tab. It has a little fun with doodling to help us think through the critical "choice points" in our journey, the decisions that have determined our life's direction.

There's a big difference between understanding the concept of having a faith story to share and having practiced sharing our faith story verbally. We move from concepts to behaviors, and we transform the idea of hospitality into the reality of hospitality: welcoming others, accepting others, establishing deep relational connections with others, and witnessing to others about our faith. Each of these is expressed through specific behaviors, and we should challenge ourselves to adopt those behaviors.

Discipleship Challenges

We are aiming to develop a lifestyle of welcome, acceptance, deep relational connections, and witnessing to our faith — a life of hospitality. While this lifestyle is not limited to any specific behavior or grouping of behaviors, it is our behaviors that form the ways that we think and engage our world:

- Identify five people with whom you have a relationship (friends, co-workers etc.) and begin to pray for an opportunity to share your faith.

- Get connected to a small group to develop a set of deeper relationships where you can be encouraged, supported, equipped, and challenged.

- Take someone to lunch. (Pick up the check.)

- Make it a point to hang out with someone who is different than you (culturally, temperamentally, or socio-economically).

Blessed . . .

While we often think about discipleship in terms of the things that we do to be faithful to God, there is another side to the discipleship coin. We are not only a blessing to others as we model Jesus' way of engaging the world; as we follow Jesus' lead and engage the world in love, we find that we ourselves are blessed in a thousand different ways. The path of hospitality to which God calls us is also the path where we will most fully experience the abundance God intends for us. In pursuing the life of hospitality, we discover the joy of deep relationships with people who care about us and want the best for us. We are challenged to grow and discover a richer life within the context of an authentic community. And we have the amazing experience of helping others connect with eternal life through a relationship with Jesus. We are blessed as we bless others.

Additional Resources You May Find Helpful

- *Shift 2.0,* by Phil Maynard (available at Excellence in Ministry Coaching's website at emc3coaching.com, as well as marketsquarebooks.com and cokesbury.com)
- *Following Jesus,* by Carolyn Slaughter
- *The Discipleship Pathway,* by Jim Harnish
- *Foundations: An Introductions to Spiritual Practices,* by Phil Maynard
- *Making Room,* by Karen Pohl

Recap for a Life of Hospitality

A life of hospitality reflects Jesus' imperative to "love our neighbor as ourselves." We experience the love and acceptance of God and the faith community, engage others as an expression of God's hospitality, and intentionally build relationships to invite others to discover God's love for them. Maturing disciples make disciples.

Supporting Scripture:

> **"Love your neighbor as yourself."**
>
> **Luke 10:47**

> **"Do to others whatever you would like them to do to you. This is the essence of all that is taught in the law and the prophets."**
>
> **Matthew 7:12**

Behaviors that reflect a life of hospitality:

- Discovering authentic community through deep relationships.

- Forgiving others and asking forgiveness.

- Supporting each other through life's challenges.

- Building relationships with those outside the faith community.

- Sharing our faith/testimony.

Questions for Reflection and Discussion

1. How have you experienced the hospitality of God through your community of faith?

2. This section describes relationships as the 'engine' that drives our witness in the community and world. On a scale of 1-10 (with 10 being the highest), how would you rate the witness of your life?

3. Who are the people your congregation is trying to reach with God's love? How are you actively involved in the lives of these people?

4. Alan Hirsch describes the sharing of meals as a "sacred practice." Who have you shared a meal with to build a deeper connection? How is this practice encouraged in your congregation?

5. Hospitality includes the practice of helping others become disciples of Jesus Christ. How are you living out the calling to "go . . . make disciples"?

6. What hospitality practice would you be willing to commit to engage this week?

CHAPTER FOUR

Becoming More Like Jesus

Becoming More Like Jesus Through a Life of Opening to God

Again, and again, we see Jesus engaging in practices that keep him connected to the Creator. He draws his power through faithfully practiced, thoughtful habits to be fully the person and the witness that God has sent him to be. We find him practicing and teaching about a wide variety of spiritual practices that sustain the God-given life:

- Prayer
- Fasting
- Generosity
- Worship
- Bible reading
- Solitude and silence
- Service

It seems that since Jesus found it beneficial to engage in these spiritual practices to maintain a relationship with God, they might also be helpful for those of us whose desire is to deepen our relationship with Jesus. The following graphic comes from the Real Discipleship Survey and shows a continuum of behaviors that one might expect to see in disciples who are acting in ways that indicate a life which is opening to God.

A LIFE OF OPENING TO GOD			
I am drawn to the story of God's love and am beginning to explore the Scriptures for myself.	I am developing a daily practice of prayer, Scripture, and devotional reading, opening myself to God.	I am exploring new spiritual disciplines and experiencing a greater level of intimacy with God.	I am taking responsibility for my own growth through the daily practice of spiritual disciplines.

These intentional spiritual practices are generally referred to as spiritual disciplines. It's in some ways unfortunate that *discipline* is the preferred terminology, since that word carries a lot of baggage in contemporary culture. But spiritual disciplines are the purposeful habits through which we experience the flow of God's grace into our lives. Grace, of course, is the gift of God's unmerited love or favor to us, and there are an unlimited number of ways to experience that outpouring of grace, from new insights about a familiar Bible passage, to a new sense of God's blessings, to a fresh idea about how to serve.

We included the following graphic in chapter two as we discussed this flow of God's grace and how it is intimately linked to intentional spiritual practices.

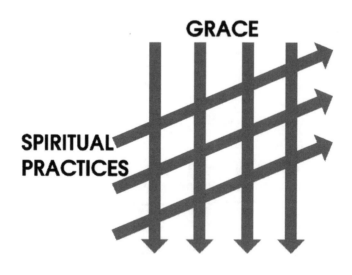

The practices we will mention have spiritual value only because of the intersection with this flow of God's grace. For example, fasting is a practice that provides the physical benefit of weight loss, but this discipline's true value for the followers of Christ is in the experience of denying ourselves in order that we might seek the presence of God and that we might find clarity in our quest for wholeness. Meditation has a variety of positive mental and physical benefits, but it is only as a spiritual discipline that it reveals deep truths from the heart of God. Prayer walks are great for getting the heart beating faster and burning calories, but as a spiritual discipline, their deeper purpose is to help us see our communities through the eyes of God.

Jesus understood and modeled the value of foundational spiritual practices/disciplines:

- **Prayer:** In the Scriptures, we read about Jesus praying some 25 times. In the teaching of the Sermon on the Mount, he encourages his disciples to engage in prayer, particularly private prayer. He gave his disciples very specific petitions to pray as he taught them how to pray (for instance, the Lord's Prayer).

- **Fasting**: As Jesus begins his public ministry, he starts with a fast in the wilderness. His ability to confront Satan is often thought to be an outcome of this spiritual preparation. Jesus also talks about fasting as if it were a normal fact of life in the religious tradition of the day.

- **Worship:** In Luke 4:16, we read that "on the Sabbath day [Jesus] went into the synagogue, as was his custom." In the fifth chapter of the Gospel of John, we read about Jesus entering Jerusalem at the time of a religious festival. While his whole life was, in fact, centered around bringing honor and glory to God (a life of worship), Jesus also modeled the value of gathering with the people of God as an expression of shared faith and spiritual growth.

- **Scripture Study and Application:** Throughout the Gospels, we encounter the phrase, "They were amazed by his teaching." The crowds were amazed. The disciples were amazed. Even the religious leaders were amazed. One of the most notable features of Jesus' life was his authority. That authority came through the knowledge and application of the Scriptures.

- **Silence and Solitude:** While Jesus regularly found himself in front of large crowds, he also made it a habit to get away from the demands of his ministry, to have regular periods of quietness and seclusion. This is a life-giving practice, especially in the context of highly demanding responsibilities or relationships.

- **Service:** As we follow the accounts of Jesus' ministry as recorded in the Gospels, his ministry of teaching was often interrupted by on-the-spot opportunities to serve. He responded to the pleas of lepers and the blind to heal them, raised Lazarus from the dead, engaged the invalid at the pool, and fed the multitudes. We sometimes miss the idea of service as a spiritual practice, but as Jesus put it in Mark 10:45, "[E]ven the Son of Man did not come to be served, but to serve. . . ."

- **Generosity:** Certainly, as we look at the sacrificial gift of his life on the cross, we see the generosity of Jesus for all of humankind. One needs only to read the Scriptures to find that this generosity was a centerpiece of Jesus' teaching and practice. One of Jesus' favorite topics is teaching about how generosity is a way of reflecting the very heart of God in stories such as the widow's mite, the Gentile who built a synagogue, and the Samaritan who took care of the injured stranger. Jesus fed the multitudes instead of sending them away. Generosity is a spiritual issue and spiritual practice.

Disciples of Jesus also find that spiritual practices like these position us in places where we experience the grace to live more fully into the lives God has called us to. These practices heighten within us a growing awareness of God's abiding presence in every moment of our day.

That's why John Wesley refers to these specific spiritual practices as Means of Grace.

Phil loves to tell the story of leading a spiritual formation retreat with a group from his local church. They were staying at a rustic motel at a conference camp, and he immediately ran into trouble:

> As we went to the assigned rooms to put our stuff away before the first group gathering, I discovered that the key to my room would not unlock the door. After trying several times unsuccessfully, my wife decided to give it a try. The door wouldn't open for her, either.
>
> Frustrated, I went back to the camp office and asked for a key that would actually open the door. They gave me a new key, and I went to try again, but I got the same result. The door just wouldn't open. As we were standing there trying to figure out what to do, Margrit (an elderly participant on the retreat) came by and asked what was going on. I replied, "This stupid door won't open, and I can't put my stuff away."
>
> Margrit asked to see the key. I thought she would do what any normal person would do and try the key in the door. But she didn't. Margrit went over and sat down on a porch swing and began to pray over the key. I thought, "What can she possibly

be praying about?" This went on for about five minutes, which, let's be honest, is a long time when you're just trying to get into your room. But then Margrit came over and put the key in the lock with a smile. And it opened on the very first try!

Phil always finishes that story by saying, "When I grow up, I want to be like Margrit!"

That is the power of spiritual practices. They open us to the working of God in our lives. Dallas Willard groups these practices into two broad but useful categories, practices of abstinence (that call on us to remove ourselves from something) and practices of engagement (which call on us to interact with something).

Disciplines of Abstinence

- **Solitude:** Intentional withdrawal from social engagement, especially for the purpose of focusing on the divine.

- **Silence:** The absence of human-created stimuli so that one can pay attention to the voice within.

- **Fasting:** Abstaining from food or other good gifts from God for spiritual purposes.

- **Frugality:** Abstinence from luxuries, behaviors, and practices for the purpose of placing control over our appetites and trusting God.

- **Chastity:** Fasting from sexual activity for the purpose of holiness.

- **Secrecy:** Finding our pleasure in God rather than in the accolades of people.

- **Sacrifice:** Giving up what we have to please God so that we may learn to rely more fully on God's providence.

Disciplines of Engagement

- **Study:** To incorporate the wisdom of God into the practices of our lives.

- **Worship:** The act of giving glory and honor to God.

- **Celebration:** Expressing joy for what God has done in our lives.

- **Service:** Giving of ourselves to promote the good of others.

- **Prayer:** Communication with God to conform our will to God.

- **Fellowship:** Engaging with other disciples and our world to experience more of God.

- **Confession:** Acknowledging our need for God's forgiveness.

- **Submission:** Freedom from the need to always have our own way. [1]

Here's a graphic that offers another way of thinking about these spiritual practices/disciplines using some different terminology. [2]

Spiritual Disciplines

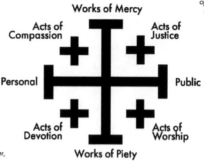

doing good works, visiting the sick, visiting those in prison, feeding the hungry, and giving generously to the needs of others

seeking justice, ending oppression and discrimination, and addressing the needs of the poor

Works of Mercy

Acts of Compassion

Acts of Justice

Personal

Public

Acts of Devotion

Acts of Worship

Works of Piety

reading, meditating and studying the scriptures, prayer, fasting, regularly attending worship, healthy living, and sharing our faith with others

regularly share in the sacraments, Christian conferencing (accountability to one another), and Bible study

The purpose of spiritual disciplines/practices is to place us in convergence with God's grace which is pouring into our world, as well as to help us develop an awareness of God's presence in our midst. Dallas Willard puts it like this:

> God is . . . seen everywhere by those who long have lived for him. No doubt God wants us to see him. That is a part of his nature as outpouring love. Love always wants to be known.

> Seeing is no simple thing, of course. Often a great deal of knowledge, experience, imagination, patience, and receptivity are required . . . . Persons rarely become present where they are not heartily wanted. . . . We prefer to be wanted, warmly wanted, before we reveal our souls . . . The ability to see and the practice of seeing God and God's world comes through a process of seeking and growing in intimacy with him.[3]

In general, when we start a spiritual practice it feels like an obligation, something we 'should' do. We all know, for example, that we 'should' pray. Perhaps this is why we spend so little time engaging in prayer. Research shows that even most pastors pray only a few minutes a day (less than five, according to the survey). We offer our obligatory thanks and maybe even a confession. Then we provide God with our laundry list of things we hope God will do for us.

What if, instead of speaking so much, we spent more time listening? Or even just being with God in silence and celebrating God's goodness? Prayer is about deepening our relationship with God. The Psalmist captures it in this passage from Psalm 8:

> **Lord, our Lord,**
> **how majestic is your name in all the earth!**
> **You have set your glory in the heavens.**
> **Through the praise of children and infants**
> **you have established a stronghold against your enemies,**
> **to silence the foe and the avenger.**
> **When I consider your heavens,**
> **the work of your fingers,**
> **the moon and the stars,**
> **which you have set in place,**
> **what is mankind that you are mindful of them,**
> **human beings that you care for them?**
>
> **Psalm 8:1-4**

And these words from Psalm 111:

> **Great are the works of the Lord;**
> **they are pondered by all who delight in them.**
> **Glorious and majestic are his deeds,**
> **and his righteousness endures forever.**
> **He has caused his wonders to be remembered;**
> **the Lord is gracious and compassionate.**
> **He provides food for those who fear him;**
> **he remembers his covenant forever.**
>
> **Psalm 111:2-5**

God is worthy of our praise, cares for us, provides for us, and is faithful to God's covenant with us forever.

Of course, not all persons will find all spiritual practices to be equally helpful. To this end, keep these guidelines in mind:

- Start small.
- Try things on for a good fit.
- Engage primarily in practices that have the greatest result.
- Keep trying new things as you keep discovering more of God.

The best way to get started is to start!

Looking at the listing of spiritual practices/disciplines presented previously, it can be overwhelming and unclear how to begin. We suggest that you consider setting aside a few minutes at some consistently scheduled time during the day to devote to growing this relationship with God (five to ten minutes to start). This personal worship time or devotional time is a common practice for disciples in all levels of maturity. It typically includes a time of prayer and a short Scripture reading and reflection. As you develop as a disciple, you may find that ten minutes does not meet your needs, and the time focused on God will need to expand. You may also discover additional spiritual disciplines that enrich that time.

Disciple Challenges

Remember that we are aiming to develop a lifestyle of placing ourselves intentionally in the path of God's grace. We are seeking to widen our awareness of God's presence. No single behavior is a perfect fit for any individual disciple, but we should work to find the behaviors, practices, and disciplines that are right for us. It is by these behaviors, practices, and disciplines that we will transform the way we think about and engage the world:

- Commit to a short daily devotional time.

- Read one of the Gospels.

- Use a resource (e.g. *Upper Room* online devotional) to guide a devotional time.

- Engage in a small group to explore more deeply the life and teachings of Jesus.

- Find a spiritual friend to journey as a disciple with you.

Blessed . . .

It is most certainly true that we bless God as we engage in spiritual practices. In a sense, this is like the development of any significant relationship where spending time with and focusing on the other person strengthens the relational connection.

It is also true that we are blessed in the process. The phrase, "They seem to have a direct line to God," is a recognition that the person being referred to has developed a keen awareness of God's presence and guidance. This state of holy connection is possible for all of us as we engage in these spiritual practices that bless and bring God's blessing.

Additional Resources You May Find Helpful

- *Foundations: An Introduction to Spiritual Practices,* by Phil Maynard (available at Excellence in Ministry Coaching's website, emc3coaching.com, as well as marketsquarebooks. com and cokesbury.com)
- *Celebration of Discipline,* by Richard Foster
- *Prayer,* by Richard Foster
- *The Divine Conspiracy,* by Dallas Willard
- *The Spirit of the Disciplines,* by Dallas Willard
- *Sacred Rhythms,* by Ruth Haley Barton
- *Discipler: An Interactive Guide to Intentional, Relational, and Accountable Discipleship,* by Phil Maynard and Eddie Pipkin (available at marketsquarebooks.com, emc3coaching.com and cokesbury.com)

Recap for a Life of Opening to God

In a life of opening to God, we intentionally place ourselves in the pathway of God's grace, receiving and acting upon the leading of God's Spirit.

Supporting Scripture:

> Since we are living by the Spirit, let us follow the Spirit's leading in every part of our lives.
>
> **Galatians 5:25**

> Trust in the Lord with all your heart; do not depend on your own understanding. Seek his will in all you do, and he will show you which path to take.
>
> **Proverbs 3:5-6**

> Do not merely listen to the word, and so deceive yourselves. Do what it says.
>
> **James 1:22**

Behaviors reflecting a life opening to God:

- Daily prayer and Scripture application.

- Exploring spiritual practices.

- Listening to God's calling in your life.

- Discerning opportunities for responding to God.

Questions for Reflection and Discussion

1. Why is it valuable for us to engage in spiritual practices/disciplines like prayer, study, fasting, and meditation?

2. What is the difference between acts of compassion and acts of justice (as referenced in the Spiritual Disciplines graphic)?

3. In what personal spiritual disciplines do you regularly engage? What have you found most helpful in your growth as a disciple?

4. As you reviewed the categories of abstinence and engagement identified by Dallas Willard, what surprised you? Do you find yourself more drawn to one category or the other?

5. In what ways have you taken responsibility for your own spiritual growth? What might be helpful to your continued development as a disciple of Jesus?

6. What might you commit to do this week to further develop as a disciple of Jesus?

Becoming More Like Jesus
Through a Life of Obeying God

Real discipleship is not about how much information we know about Jesus. It is about how much we are living like Jesus. (Or as we said in an earlier chapter, it's not just information; it's transformation.)

A life of obeying God is a life that sees the world as Jesus sees the world, responds to the world as Jesus would respond, and *pours itself* into the world to partner with Jesus in helping people everywhere discover the Kingdom life God intended. The essence of this dimension of the journey of discipleship is steady growth as we become more and more like Jesus — taking in information and inspiration and churning out practical applications through action. It's designed to be a lifelong, open-ended journey. This is the part where we fully embrace John Wesley's challenge of "going on to perfection."

The Apostle Paul presents the challenge in the fourth chapter of Ephesians:

> [U]ntil we every one . . . grow up to be perfect in the maturity of the fullness of Christ; so that we henceforth would no longer be children, wavering and carried with every wind of doctrine by the wiliness of men, and craftiness whereby they lay in wait for us, to deceive us.
>
> But let us follow the truth in love, and in all things grow in him who is the head; that is to say, Christ.
>
> **Ephesians 4:13-15 (New Matthew Bible)**

This is the same idea expressed earlier as we quoted Jesus when he said, "Be perfect, therefore, as your heavenly father is perfect" (Matthew 5:48). It's the same idea that drove John

91

Wesley's fixation on accountability, the drive to be continuously improving.

A life obeying God is about 'growing up,' and we move from infancy towards maturity by gaining a deeper and deeper understanding of the life and teachings of Jesus, and then actively putting what we have learned into practice. The following graphic from the Real Discipleship Survey displays a continuum of behaviors that reflect a life that is growing in obedience to Jesus.

A LIFE OF OBEYING GOD			
I understand more about Jesus' teaching through Bible Study classes and my own reading.	I have accepted the call to be a follower of Jesus Christ and am committed to being part of the church, becoming like Jesus, and serving others.	I am daily seeking to apply the teaching of Scripture to my own life.	I am partnering with God to help others grow in openness and obedience to Christ.

As we examine the life of Jesus, there is no shortage of fascinating facets to explore. Inevitably, though, whatever sub-topic of Jesus' teachings we choose for our focus, we find that the foundation of that teaching is always built on Jesus' profound understanding of Scripture. It formed his philosophy, his core values, and his code of conduct. Scripture was the primer by which Jesus determined how to carry out God the Father's mission of loving and redeeming the world. Jesus' sacred text was, of course, the Hebrew Scriptures, what we now refer to as the Old Testament. Even as a child of about twelve years of age, Jesus astounded the teachers with his command and understanding of God's Word. In Luke 2:47, after he had spent three days in the temple courts, here was the report: "Everyone who heard him was amazed at his understanding and his answers." Such eyewitness accounts of astonishment by those who heard him are a recurrent theme of the Gospels.

Jesus knew the Scriptures. Jesus understood the context and history of the Scriptures. Jesus applied the Scriptures to daily life. Jesus taught the Scriptures to all who would listen, opening the eyes of the people to new ways of understanding familiar words. Jesus discipled others to help them understand and live into the guidance of the Scriptures, God's instructions for life, the glorious narrative of God's redeeming love for God's people, and the repository of God's promises for all who would follow his ways.

Knowing these precious words and absorbing them in our hearts, minds, and souls: this is a life of obeying God.

Jesus, says repeatedly, with an understanding of Kingdom life that sprouts forth from its roots in the Hebrew Scriptures, "You have heard it said . . . but I say to you . . . " The New Testament recounts these words and teachings and the events from the life and ministry of Jesus (the Gospels). The rest of the New Testament records the impact of those events and teachings on an emerging world, shaped by the acts of the Apostles (the sent ones of Jesus). If we are serious about our discipleship, we will familiarize ourselves with this holy record and work to understand these events and obey these teachings. And we won't stop with our own edification. We'll help others along this path, too, because disciples do what Jesus said, and Jesus proclaimed, "Go, therefore, and make disciples."

There is, however, too often a disturbing disconnect between the allegiance people profess to the Bible and their actual commitment to knowing, understanding, and obeying its principles and precepts. Greg Ogden, in *Transforming Discipleship,* highlights the research of the Gallup and Barna organizations related to the Scriptures:

Gallup has written, "Americans revere the Bible — but, by and large, they don't read it." According to Gallup, 65 percent of the adult population agree that the Bible "answers all or most of the basic questions of life." Barna's surveys found that 60 percent of all American adults and 85 percent who described themselves as born again would affirm the statement "The Bible is totally accurate in all that it teaches." In spite of these affirmations there is an appalling ignorance of the book we put on a pedestal. For example, 53 percent of the adults in Barna's survey believed that the saying "God helps those who help themselves" is a biblical truth. [4]

Barna, himself, notes this dissonance in his work, *Maximum Faith:*

> [T]o assist you in that journey (toward spiritual wholeness), He (God) provides a role model (Jesus Christ), a 24/7 advisor (the Holy Spirit), an exhaustive but nontechnical document containing the critical plans, operating principles and performance metrics (the Bible), and a support group (the Church). If you use those resources appropriately, you will experience the kind of redefined life He (God) has promised.
>
> But in a stunning display of either arrogance or ignorance — or perhaps both — we consistently choose different role models, ignore our consultant, fail to read the manual, pursue our personal preferences and measures, and refuse the input and accountability available from the support group. [5]

A classic example of this is represented by the mountain of debt that a significant portion of our society has buried itself under. Falling prey to the materialism, consumerism, and easy debt around us, we use our credit cards to buy stuff we don't need with money we don't have. If only we had read (and followed) God's how-to manual:

> **The rich rule over the poor, and the borrower is servant to the lender.**
>
> **Proverbs 22:7**

> **I have learned the secret of being content in any and every situation, whether well-fed or hungry, whether living in plenty or in want.**
>
> **Philippians 4:12**

> **Owe nothing to anyone, except to love one another.**
>
> **Romans 13:8**

So, if we want to live differently than the culture around us which bombards us with relentless messages 24 hours a day, how do we go about developing this life of obedience — obeying God?

First, if you haven't already developed this most elemental of Christ-following habits, begin by reading the Bible day by day, a little bit at a time. It is beneficial to read more than a single, cherry-picked verse, because it is too easy to take an individual verse out of context. Read instead by chapters or topical chunks. This method promotes reading that focuses on a coherent unit or thought. We encourage people to begin their reading — especially if it's a new thing they're trying — with the Gospels. Be sure to use a version of the Scriptures that is easy for you to read and understand. Below is a comparison of several versions using a familiar passage, the fourth verse of the 23rd Psalm:

- **New International Version** (easy to read/good translation): "Even though I walk through the darkest valley, I will fear no evil, for you are with me; your rod and your staff, they comfort me."

- **New American Standard Version** (closest to the Greek text): "Even though I walk through the valley of the shadow of death, I fear no evil, for You are with me; Your rod and Your staff, they comfort me."

- **New Revised Standard Version** (inclusive language): "Even though I walk through the darkest valley, I fear no evil; for you are with me; your rod and your staff — they comfort me."

- *The Message* (a highly idiomatic translation in contemporary language, very readable, very poetic): "Even when the way goes through Death Valley, I'm not afraid when you walk at my side. Your trusty shepherd's crook makes me feel secure."

- **King James Version** (the "authorized" standard for over 200 years): "Yea, though I walk through the valley of the shadow of death, I will fear no evil: for thou art with me; thy rod and thy staff they comfort me."

  The King James Version of the Bible (the KJV), the English Bible relied on by Protestants for centuries, features flowing, elaborate language that influenced literature for 400 years. Filled with plenty of "thees" and "thous," it makes for very beautiful reading, if perhaps confusing comprehension. There are many who still prefer to memorize passages from this version (especially poetic passages like the 23rd Psalm that they first heard in the language of sixteenth century England).

Now there are dozens of translations and paraphrases available, and most of them are accessible online for free through sites such as biblegateway.com. Find one that feels comfortable for you. It is also very enlightening to compare various translations head-to-head in order to glean different insights from the different versions, a process that modern technology has made easy.

Second, discover some basic techniques for reading and studying the Scriptures:

- **Theological Bible Study:** Study the passage by asking three questions:
  - What does this text say about God?
  - What does this text say about humankind?
  - What does this text say about the relationship between God and humankind?

- **Reflective Bible Study:** This approach to the Scriptures invites the text to be read two to three times and then to identify a word or phrase from the text that speaks to you. This word or phrase becomes a focus of reflection, seeking wisdom from God.

- **Praying the Scriptures:** Use the phraseology of the Scripture passage as a focus of personal prayers. For example, a commonly used phrase from John 3:16, "whoever believes" or "whosoever believes," can become a personalized prayer version of that Scripture. "For God so loved the world that he gave his one and only Son, that whoever believes in him shall not perish but have eternal life" becomes "For God so loved the world that he gave his one and only Son, that Eddie, who believes in him, shall not perish. . . ."

- **SOAP Method:** This is a journaling tool which uses the following format:
  - Scripture reading.
  - Observations about the passage.

  ◦ Application to your life.

  ◦ Prayer related to living into the passage.

- **The Journalist's Questions:** This approach asks the questions Who, What, When, Where, Why, and How about the text.

Third, take advantage of the many options for Bible study materials. There are, quite literally, thousands of professionally written Bible studies available for those who want to grow closer to Christ:

- Booklets for use by one person, for small groups, or for large groups.

- Daily devotionals that use Scripture, prayer, and reflections for daily inspiration.

- Guides that can lead you through the whole Bible in one year, two years, three years, or more.

- Booklets that explore one book of the Bible.

- Study guides that are gender-based, affinity-based, or tied to various seasons of life (e.g. men's Bible studies, women's Bible studies, youth Bible studies, children's Bible studies, studies for married couples, studies for parents, studies for those who have retired, studies for cancer survivors, etc.).

- Guides in different languages.

- Booklets for different ethnicities.

- Booklets on different topics in the Bible.

- Studies for seasons of the year, like Easter, Christmas, or Advent.

- Studies for people with disabilities or for their families.

- Guides for people struggling with addiction or other problems.

- Bible studies for people who are called to work with the poor or oppressed, addicts, or the homeless.

- Studies for those who are called to evangelize.

- Studies for those who want to see their church grow and develop.

Fourth, become familiar with commentaries on the Bible. These are typically written by biblical scholars and include some helpful information in understanding the Scriptures, such as historical context, geographic practices, religious traditions, demographic understandings, and even word studies. Look up Bible commentaries on the internet, and a wide variety of resources are available for any selected passage. Review and compare several sources to identify common themes. There are even sources that take you back to the original language and can help you understand some of the nuances.

Fifth, write down insights from the messages offered during worship services. Pastors and teachers have often done much of the research around a specific passage and can be a great guide for deeper understanding.

Sixth, reflect on what is being discovered in any Scripture passage you read. How does it apply to your life? How might you behave differently if you did what the Scripture invited? This is often the missing component in the study of Scripture. As an example, Phil is currently participating in a video conference Bible study on the book of Philippians. There's been a lot

of conversation about where Philippi is located and its significance in the biblical world. Paul's circumstance of writing
from prison has been noted, along with some discussion about
what happened to put him there and even where the prison is
located. The presenter, a noted biblical scholar, has taken a
deep dive into some of the Greek words in the text and explored
the nuances of meaning that might result. These are all great
things to do in a Bible study. But Phil's still waiting for the part
where there is discussion about how he might live differently
this week, based on what he's discovering about this passage
in the Word. How do we apply what we've been so extensively
studying? This is the true purpose of Bible study. Discipleship
is about transformation, not information.

Seventh, study the Scriptures with a small group of friends.
Share insights. Challenge one another. Hold one another
accountable. John Wesley believed we understand Scripture
only with an invitation of the Holy Spirit to reveal its truths
to us. He famously said that even "the devils" acknowledged
the Scriptures, but they never receive the truth and act upon it
for their own growth and edification. Wesley believed that the
Bible was best read "in conference" with others. This is why
Bible reading was an unwavering part of every Society, Class,
and Band meeting. It is important to surround ourselves with
the wisdom of others who have been engaged in Scripture study
for longer than we have (as well as life experience filtered
through an application of the Scriptures).

Disciple Challenges

Remember, our goal is not to only read the Scriptures, as
beneficial as that activity can be. The outcome we are seeking as

we engage this dimension of spiritual development is that we are living a life of obedience to what we are studying. It is the behaviors that we begin because of our study that transform our attitudes and engagement with the world:

- Commit to a daily time of reading and reflecting on the Scriptures.
- Engage in a small group to explore more deeply the life and teachings of Jesus.
- Find a spiritual friend to journey as a disciple with you.

Blessed . . .

It is most certainly true that we bless God as we commit to engage in spiritual practices. In a sense this is like the development of any significant relationship where spending time and focusing on the other person strengthens the relational connection.

It is also true that we are blessed in the process. As we begin to dig into the truths of the Bible, we discover that God has ordained a particular way of doing life that brings a sense of peace, fulfillment, and hope to a chaotic world. As we do what the Scriptures instruct, we discover that a life lived as God intends is also a blessed life. For example, when we learn how to use the financial resources God has provided in the ways that God intends, we discover that we are no longer bound by the chains of the slavery of debt, we are no longer fearful about our basic needs being met, we find contentment in what God has provided, and we are able to bless others more.

Additional Resources You May Find Helpful

- *Foundations: An Introduction to Spiritual Practices,* by Phil Maynard (available at the Excellence in Ministry website at emc3coaching.com, as well as marketsquarebooks.com and cokesbury.com)

- *Thinking Like Jesus,* by George Barna

- *Discipler: An Interactive Guide to Intentional, Relational, and Accountable Discipleship,* by Phil Maynard and Eddie Pipkin

- *Maximum Faith,* by George Barna

- *The Divine Conspiracy,* by Dallas Willard

Recap of the Life of Obeying God

A life of obeying God is a life centered around the knowledge, understanding, and application of the Scriptures to daily life. It includes actually doing what the Word of God instructs us to do.

Supporting Scripture:

> **All Scripture is God-breathed and is useful for instruction, for conviction, for correction, and for training in righteousness, so that the man of God may be complete, fully equipped for every good work. . . .**
>
> **2 timothy 3:16-17**

> **Thy Word is a lamp unto my feet and a light unto my path.**
>
> **Psalm 119:105**

Behaviors reflecting a life obeying God:

- Daily study of the Scriptures.

- Journaling about what we're learning and how we're applying it.

- Obedience to the Word of God (doing what it says, just like Jesus did).

Questions for Reflection and Discussion

1. George Barna writes, "We consistently choose different role models, ignore our consultant, fail to read the manual, pursue our personal preferences and measures, and refuse the input and accountability available from support groups." How well do you think this describes your congregation?

2. Which of the following are not from the Bible? Circle your selections.

Money is the root of all evil.

This too shall pass.

Cleanliness is next to Godliness.

God works in mysterious ways.

Be in the world, but not of the world.

God will not give you more than you can handle.

3. As a group, try the SOAP Method (a journaling tool) for the Scripture passage John 1:1-14.

    a. Scripture (John 1:1-14)

    b. Observations

    c. Application

    d. Prayer based on observations and application

4. For the same passage try the Journalist's approach. Answer the Who, What, When, Where, Why, & How questions.

5. What practices have you found most helpful for studying and applying Scripture to life?

6. Obeying God includes doing what we are told. How are you living into the imperative to "Go, therefore, and make disciples"?

CHAPTER FIVE

Blessing the World

Blessing the World Through a Life of Service

Central to the faith journey of a disciple of Jesus Christ is the call to serve others. The concept of service has always been at the core of the identity of the people of God who, from the beginning, were called to be a "blessing to the nations."

It is through serving others that we become expressions of God's love for the world. It is through serving others that we make a difference in the lives of people whom God loves (thereby communicating the message as God's hands and feet in action that those people are, in fact, loved). It is through serving others that we help the world to discover what it means to bring forth "thy Kingdom come, on earth as it is in heaven."

The Scriptures are clear that every person has been gifted and called by God to selflessly and sacrificially serve others.

It is also clear that the Church exists not for itself but for the community it is called to serve. A life of service is a growth in grace toward joining Jesus in mission to the world, using the gifts, passions, and talents with which we have each been uniquely blessed.

Jesus himself modeled this life of service. Service is an expression of God's love for God's people. Jesus sums this all up in John 15:

"This is my commandment, that you love one another as I have loved you. Greater love has no one than this, that he lay down his life for his friends."

John 15:12-13

While this heart for serving others is most dramatically illustrated in Jesus' sacrifice of his life on a cross, there is much more to the story. Jesus served selflessly and sacrificially in a thousand different ways, long before his experience on the cross. Service means to engage other people in ways that are life-giving, that meet identified needs, and that raise those people up. Service, done best and exemplified by Jesus, means establishing a personal connection, focusing on the relational aspect of the interaction. Service is ultimately not about the thing being done to meet a need, but about relationships between people.

Jesus was the master at serving in the moment as an opportunity presented itself. In his responsiveness to human need in real time, he modeled for us what it means to serve:

- Jesus fed the hungry.

- Jesus confronted the religious establishment that was taking advantage of the poor.

- Jesus comforted the grieving.

- Jesus healed the sick.

- Jesus cared for the mentally ill.

- Jesus raised the dead.

- Jesus washed his disciples' feet.

Jesus spells it out for us:

"I have set an example for you, that you should do as I have done for you."

John 13:15

The following excerpt from the Real Discipleship Survey tracks a continuum of behaviors and attitudes that demonstrate our progression toward a life of Christlike service.

A LIFE OF SERVICE			
I am often amazed at the way some disciples selflessly serve others and I want to make a difference as well.	I know Christ invites me to join him in serving others and I'm discovering how God has gifted me to do this.	I experiment with serving in different areas as I discover my gifts, talents, and passions.	I join Jesus in mission to others using my God-given gifts, talents, and passions.

Disciples of Jesus seek to live into this calling of a life of service. So how do we get started?

Sometimes we are surprised to learn that even long-time church folk don't make the connection between discipleship and service. One of Phil's former partners in congregational development was visiting a local church to teach about discipleship during their Sunday worship. Afterwards, as the people filed out of the building, an elderly gentleman stopped and said, "When did the rules get changed?"

Phil's friend responded, "What rules are you talking about?"

The man said, "I've been going to this church for nearly fifty years, and nobody has ever told me before that to be a disciple I have to serve people."

Is it possible for someone to attend church for fifty years and never hear a message about serving others? Maybe he spent decades sleeping through those parts! Or maybe our leaders aren't clearly presenting a teaching about which Jesus was always crystal clear: To follow is to serve. Regularly. Enthusiastically. Putting others first.

Service to others is inseparable from discipleship. The whole point of all that internal work of opening to God and obeying God is arguably to prepare us for service. It is also important to understand that service done as Jesus did it means that we actually connect with those being served. Lots of people do things that they call service (e.g. giving things to people, donating to causes) that are not really service. They are acts of generosity — and generosity is also beneficial (as you'll see in the section that comes next), but generosity can be undertaken from afar, as opposed to the intimacy of offering ourselves to others at close range as Jesus did. The root word of *service* is *serve,* and to serve you actually have to engage people. It's a hands-on process.

A significant step into living a life of service is discovering how it is that God has 'wired' you to serve. While there are many ways to do our part, it is an important biblical truth that God has gifted us for service differently, each way of serving valuable, and each needed. Many congregations have people take a spiritual gifts inventory as a step in this process. This is a popular kind of questionnaire in church circles, which is based on identifying a person's specific gifts, as specified by Scripture, that are provided by God through the Holy Spirit. These gifts are described by the Apostle Paul:

> **There are different kinds of gifts, but the same Spirit distributes them. There are different kinds of service, but the same Lord. There are different kinds of working, but in all of them and in everyone it is the same God at work.**

Now to each one the manifestation of the Spirit is given
for the common good. To one there is given through
the Spirit a message of wisdom, to another a message
of knowledge by means of the same Spirit, to another
faith by the same Spirit, to another gifts of healing by
that one Spirit, to another miraculous powers, to another
prophecy, to another distinguishing between spirits, to
another speaking in different kinds of tongues, and to
still another the interpretation of tongues. All these are
the work of one and the same Spirit, and he distributes
them to each one, just as he determines.

I Corinthians 12:4-11

Knowing our spiritual gifts can be helpful and give us
direction in seeking a place to serve, but we are more than our
spiritual gifts. A more comprehensive approach guides Rick
Warren's S.H.A.P.E. resource (from Saddleback Community
Church), which does a nice job of helping us understand a more
complete gifting for service. God can use the totality of who we
are in the service of the Kingdom. For example, many of us have
skills that result from our education, training, careers, and
even hobbies. All of us have a variety of life experiences that
form our abilities to engage in Kingdom work. We even have
different personality types. All of these parts of our story can
be of significant value in making a difference in people's lives
and in our world. The following graphic summarizes Warren's
process.[1]

S	What are your spiritual gifts, the capacities or strengths with which others have recognized you making a difference and being a blessing to them?
H	What strums your heart strings? What are your interests, your passions, the things about which you care deeply?
A	What are your abilities, the things you do well, that you do naturally or have learned over time to do? What assets do you have that enable you to do certain things?
P	What is your personality? How has God wired you?
E	What experiences have equipped you to gain knowledge, strength, or perspective that can be a blessing to others?

Eric Rees, S.H.A.P.E. (adapted), Zondervan Publishing, 2006.

This tool honors the importance of spiritual gifts, but it also takes in other valuable contributing factors when considering how God can use your gifting as you serve others.

Many churches offer this gifting discernment process as part of a Discipleship Pathway program for the congregation. The Discipleship Pathway is an intentional process for helping disciples grow in all the areas we've discussed of becoming more like Jesus. It typically includes a focus on meeting people where they are in their discipleship journey, intentional training, and educational support to help them move forward on that journey, and partnerships to facilitate growth. We highly recommend that when you have completed the discernment process (whatever that process looks like for you in your local context), you have a conversation with an experienced leader from the congregation about how your particular gift mix might be a strong match with opportunities to serve.

Some years ago, Phil forged an unlikely connection with Peter, a retired contractor from the U.S. who was living in Jamaica and building homes for expats in that country. Peter was a lapsed Catholic who was a little rough around the edges — colorful, shall we say. Phil was doing some local mission work with a team and Peter stopped by to see what they were working on. He immediately became interested in helping out, and that interest, as he built a relationship with Phil and others on the team, grew to a passion for the work they were doing. So, over the years, as Phil organized mission teams to Jamaica, Peter would take a week off from his regular job and work with the mission teams to make sure they knew how to do the construction work, had the right tools, and knew where to locate the needed materials.

Together, Phil, Peter, and teams of traveling disciples from the United States renovated Jamaican structures to be community centers, built additions to churches, and repaired school roofs. God used Peter to make a difference in communities drawing on skills he had developed over a career as a builder. Peter had never completed a comprehensive course of Bible study (or a spiritual gifts inventory for that matter), but God found a high-impact way to use him and his skill set.

If we over-compartmentalize our thinking about how God can use our gifts, we miss opportunities to serve. This is true if we pigeonhole our unique combination of skills, gifts, and passions (or allow others to do the pigeonholing for us, as often happens). It is also true if we get into the rut of thinking that our service only counts if it is organized and supervised by our local congregation. Service does not have to be grandiose or sponsored by the institutional church for it to be Christlike and meaningful. These things also count:

- Fixing dinner for a family in need.
- Taking a neighbor to the doctor.
- Mowing a neighbor's lawn when they are sick.
- Taking care of a neighbor's children in a time of crisis.
- Watching your neighbor's pet while they are away.
- Supporting a Habitat for Humanity project.
- Giving a couple of hours serving at the local soup kitchen.
- Mentoring a high school student.
- Reading with an elementary school student.
- Make a list of your own service experiences or potential ideas for ways to serve. Be creative. Try to think of things beyond the familiar options.

As we noted earlier, one of the amazing things about Jesus' ministry is the way he made himself available in the moment to meet the immediate needs of those around him. He saw the need, and he responded to it. As you begin to discern how God has gifted you to serve others, it is suggested that you 'try on' some different ways of serving to determine what seems to be a good fit.

As you get more and more comfortable with a particular way of engaging in service, you are encouraged to make this a way of life. Responding to the immediate needs of people is an aspect of **mercy ministries.** These service ministries address people's physical necessities. One of the outcomes of serving regularly to meet those needs is that we eventually find ourselves considering not only how to solve the crisis of the moment, but how we might address the larger social and political systems that caused those needs in the first place. If we act on that impulse to solve the larger societal and institutional issues by working to affect policy, this is called being involved in **justice ministries.**

For example, one might discover a calling to help meet the nutritional needs of lower income families that are finding it difficult to put food on the table every day. You might support a local food bank, conduct food drives, or help families in the community develop an awareness of available services. Then you begin to realize that the issue is bigger than just having access to some extra food to stretch the budget month to month. You might feel called to help those families learn how to manage their finances so they can stretch their budget farther and have less need for outside help. You might feel called to train people in interview or resume writing skills, so they have a stronger chance to land a higher paying job. You might feel called to lobby the local government to increase the minimum wage so that families might earn a living wage. These efforts to "not just give a person a fish but teach that person how to fish" and level the playing field for all fishing people everywhere are examples of justice ministries.

Phil worked with a church in southeastern Florida that was receiving a significant number of requests for assistance with home repairs and lawn care. It turned out that this mysterious increase in calls for help were the direct result of the city commission creating an ordinance fining people whose homes needed attention. Most of the affected people were senior citizens with limited resources and limited physical capabilities. The church immediately responded by mowing a lot of lawns. But members of that church, in partnership with a host of other churches from many different denominations, petitioned the city leaders to adjust the ordinance. This is an example of a move from mercy ministry to justice ministry.

Disciple Challenges

Remember that the goal here is not just to check service off your to-do list, either by serving in your local church or even in a community program. The goal is that we are building relationships through our service and that we are using the gifts and experiences God has given us to have a long-term commitment to sacrificially offering ourselves to others:

- Find a way to serve in your local church where you get to make a contribution to the life and ministry of your congregation.
- Take a course in discerning how God has 'wired' you to serve in the Kingdom.
- Find a way to serve someone in need each week.

Blessed . . .

It is most certainly true that we bless God and others as we commit to engage in a life of service. In a sense, this is like the development of any significant relationship where spending time and focus on the other person strengthens the relational connection.

It is also true that we are blessed in the process. One of the great joys of the discipleship journey is the experience of God using you to make a difference in someone's life.

Additional Resources You May Find Helpful

- *Shift 2.0,* by Phil Maynard (available at the Excellence in Ministry Coaching website at emc3coaching.com, as well as marketsquarebooks.com and cokesbury.com)
- *Outreach,* by Group Ministries
- *The Externally Focused Church,* by Rick Rusaw and Eric Swanson
- *When Helping Hurts,* by Steve Corbett and Brian Fikkert
- *What Every Church Member Should Know about Poverty,* by Bill Ehlig and Ruby K. Payne
- *Foundations: An Introduction to Spiritual Practices,* by Phil Maynard
- *S.H.A.P.E.,* by Eric Rees.

Recap for a Life of Service

Living a life of service means that we are responsive to the needs that God places in our path and seek to support those in need (mercy ministries). We also address the systems that result in producing those needs (justice ministries).

Supporting Scripture:

> For we are God's masterpiece. He has created us anew in Christ Jesus, so we can do the good things he planned for us long ago.
>
> **Ephesians 2:10**

> Their only suggestion was that we keep on helping the poor, which I have always been eager to do.
>
> **Galatians 2:10**

Behaviors reflecting a life of service:

- Discerning how God has 'wired' us for serving others.
- Blessing others with our words and deeds.
- Ministry to the poor and needy.
- Speaking up for people experiencing injustice.

Questions for Reflection and Discussion

1. What is the difference between mercy ministries and justice ministries?

2. The chapter suggests that 'service' means to actually 'serve,' which means that we must relationally engage the person being served. How are you engaged in serving in this way?

3. What is your S.H.A.P.E.? What insights might your friends bring to this understanding?

4. How have you helped someone in need this week?

5. What strikes you about the idea that "the church exists not for itself but for the community it is called to serve"?

6. What are some ways your congregation is involved in serving the surrounding community?

7. What might you do this week to develop the practice of a life of service?

Blessing the World
Through a Life of Generosity

Disciples are called to be extravagantly generous people. This includes our time, our energies, and our financial resources. The generosity of our time and energies was included in the exploration of a life of service. In this chapter, we focus on the use of our financial resources.

In a culture that struggles with what has often been referred to as *affluenza* (the disease of consumerism and materialism that is eating away at our lives), a powerful antidote can be found in a life of generosity. A life of generosity reminds us that our worth comes not from what we have, but from whose we are. It weans us away from a dependence on material things and frees us to be responsive to how we might be used by God to transform the world and make a difference in the lives of others less fortunate than ourselves.

A life of generosity is a movement of God's grace that invites us to discover that our role, regarding financial resources and material blessings, is to act as faithful managers of what God has provided. Such faithfulness on our part blesses others, and it blesses us, too (with a new level of gratitude, a deeper understanding of trust, and a profound sense of peace and contentment).

Jesus' very birth into this world (the Incarnation) was an expression of God's generosity. Many of us memorized what is perhaps the most well-known of all Bible verses, John 3:16, "For God so loved the world that he **gave** his one and only Son, that whoever believes in him shall not perish but have eternal life." God gives. Jesus is history's fullest expression of that munificence.

Jesus lived and taught about a life of generosity:

- Jesus was generous with his time and energy.
- Jesus was generous with his gifts.
- Jesus was generous in providing for the needs of others.
- Jesus taught about generosity as a way of being.

This graphic from the Real Discipleship Survey shows a continuum of behaviors representing the movement of disciples toward becoming more like Jesus in relation to stewardship of financial resources.

A LIFE OF GENEROSITY			
I give some when I attend worship.	I am giving more and more regularly.	I am tithing and reconsidering how I spend the other 90%.	I am tithing and consciously reordering my life to free up more resources to honor God and bless others.

Disciples of Jesus seek to grow into this life of generosity.

So, how do we get started?

As a spiritual practice of generosity, many people begin to give of their resources initially when they come to a worship experience, because they look around and see this practice modeled by others in attendance. In a sense this might feel like an obligation, even as if we are paying for the privilege of being there or to meet our share of the expenses of the event. Generosity, though, is not about a sense of obligation. It is a matter of the heart and a matter of rightly understanding our relationship with God and all that God has provided for us.

Generosity flows out of an understanding that God is the provider of all things and the owner of everything we have.

We are the managers or stewards of what God has provided. As the owner, God has the right to everything we have. As the stewards or managers of those resources, we are accountable to God for their responsible use. Being thoughtful about this process reinforces important truths about the values God seeks to inculcate within us:

- **Thankfulness:** "Enter his gates with thanksgiving and his courts with praise" (Psalm 100:4).

- **Contentment:** "I know what it is to be in need, and I know what it is to have plenty. I have learned the secret of being content in any and every situation, whether well fed or hungry, whether living in plenty or in want. I can do everything through him who gives me strength" (Philippians 4:12).

- **Compassion:** "Then the righteous will answer him, 'Lord, when did we see you hungry and feed you, or thirsty and give you something to drink? When did we see you a stranger and invite you in, or needing clothes and clothe you? When did we see you sick or in prison and go to visit you?' The king will reply, 'Truly I tell you, whatever you did for one of the least of these brothers and sisters of mine, you did for me'" (Matthew 25:37-40).

- **Liberality:** "The next day he took out two denarii and gave them to the innkeeper. 'Look after him,' he said, 'and when I return, I will reimburse you for any extra expense you may have'" (Luke 10:35).

God provides not only for our needs but also uses us to meet the needs of those less fortunate than we are. This is generosity. It is living on less than what God provides so that we can bless others more. This concept of living on less than what

God has provided is called "living within financial margins" by professional financial advisors. It is not a new idea. In fact, it has been around for thousands of years. Consider this ancient instruction from the Hebrew Scriptures in the book of Leviticus:

> **When you reap the harvest of your land, do not reap to the very edges of your field or gather the gleanings of your harvest. Do not go over your vineyard a second time or pick up the grapes that have fallen. Leave them for the poor and the foreigner.**
>
> **Leviticus 19:9-10**

The Hebrew people were literally instructed to live within margins. This living within margins was originally designed for the specific purpose of providing for the needs of those less fortunate. It is God's way of taking care of all the people. It is also God's way of teaching us that all that we have is from God and belongs to God.

Often, our movement toward a life of generosity begins with giving regularly to the ministries of our local congregation. The local church offers significant opportunities to make a difference in the surrounding community. We support those efforts through our regular giving. While this giving does not relieve us of the call to meet specific needs God places in our path, it does give us the opportunity to be part of something bigger than ourselves. Amazing ministries are providing for the needs of people in our communities and all around the world that would not be possible through our individual resources working alone. Wells are being dug to provide clean drinking water, hospitals are being funded to care for the sick, food is being distributed to feed the hungry, and shelters are being constructed to house the less fortunate. We, through our giving, have an opportunity to support this kind of difference-making in the world.

As we grow toward maturity, we begin to live into the biblical mandate of bringing our tithes. A tithe is 10% of what God has provided. While this may seem like a lot, it is really an ideal amount, just enough to make a difference in both our lives and the lives of those in need. To put it into perspective, consider the image of cutting an apple into 10 slices. Then set one slice aside to help feed someone else. You still have most of the apple to meet your needs and stave off your hunger. That's the way God intends for us to use the resources God has provided.

Generosity moves us from "spoon" to "ladle" thinking:

> [A] spoon is for feeding yourself, but a ladle is for serving others. The "spoon" vs "ladle" thinking illustrates a mindset that is counterculture. When we give up our spoon and pick up a ladle, we are following the example of Christ by choosing to think of others' needs ahead of our own. This kind of generosity does not come easily and always moves us beyond our comfort zone. For some, "ladle thinking" does mean writing a check, while for others, it involves inviting someone into their life or taking the time to serve another person. "Ladle thinking" requires faith and dependence on Christ. The "ladle" can manifest itself in different ways, but it always involves a putting off of selfish desires and a dependence on Christ. [2]

The goal of a life of generosity, however, is not tied to a specific amount that we are to give. It is about a lifestyle where we choose to live on less than God has provided — the part where we live within our margins — so that we may free up resources to be used for blessing others. It is also not about exclusively supporting the institutional church. A life of generosity is about living in such a way that we are ready to respond when God gives us opportunities unique to our context and setting.

A couple of years ago, Phil had one of those moments:

My younger brother was a truck driver (part of a husband and wife long-distance trucking team). He had been unable to work due to an accident. As he was struggling his way through the bureaucracy, seeking disability support, his money ran out. It was January, and he and his wife were living in a camper shell on the back of his pickup truck. They were renting a space in a campground in Wisconsin. He called me (a rare event) and said, "I don't know how we're going to pay the campground fees or put food on the table starting next week. Is there any way you can help?"

I replied that I could and would. Then I called my dad and lined him up to help as well. Between the two of us, we got them through a difficult time.

Phil points out that none of this would have been possible if he and Becky had not embraced the strategy of living within financial margins: "If we had spent everything God had blessed us with as soon as it came in, we would have had no option to help." Choosing to live a life of generosity means choosing to put aside our own desires to bless others more. Michael Slaughter puts it like this:

You and I are the only bank account that Jesus has to carry

out his mission in the world. I get tired of hearing people ask, "How can a loving God let innocent children suffer and starve?" God doesn't; God's people do. A disciple chooses to follow Jesus in living more simply so that others may simply live. [3]

As we noted back in chapter two, John Wesley, suggested the following easy-to-remember rules for managing our financial resources:

• Earn all you can.

• Save all you can.

• Give all you can.

He fleshed these principles out more fully in a sermon titled, "The Use of Money." In encouraging his flock to earn all they could, he stressed the values of hard work in the service of godly principles, not attaining money by any nefarious means possible, but by working honestly and serving others with integrity and compassion. That way they might gain all the material resources within their capabilities, but never at the expense of the welfare of other human beings.

In challenging his fellow disciples to save all they could, he was not an advocate for hoarding our wealth or even locking large sums away in grand investment schemes in anticipation of some glamorous future retirement. He was preaching about living a frugal lifestyle. He believed in setting as much as possible aside by saying a firm "no" to materialism and waste. And the purpose of those savings was not to finance living large in our golden years. The purpose was to fund more generous giving.

In encouraging his fellow disciples to give all they could, he showed how the earning and saving we discipline ourselves to do then empowers us to live generously, because living generously is how our lives reflect God's character in the world. God is generous. Therefore, we are generous as an acknowledgment and response to that divine template.

Disciple Challenges

Remember, the goal is not just to give some cash to the church or even to support a community ministry. The outcome for which we are working is that we are living a comprehensive life of generosity, allowing God to use us in ways that demonstrate trust, hope, and love. It is through specific behaviors that we form our life-changing habits of generosity:

- Find a way to give of your resources, your time, and your energies in your local church so that you get to make a meaningful partnership contribution to the life and ministry of your congregation and support its initiatives to change the world.
- Take a course in biblical principles for financial management.
- Find a way to provide for a need in your community.

Blessed ...

We bless God and others as we engage in a life of generosity. Whether it is providing a meal for someone who is hungry, shelter for someone without a home, or resources to get someone back to the home they have, we bless God when we are faithful with the resources God has provided.

It is also true that we are blessed in the process. One of the great joys of the discipleship journey is the experience of being used by God to make a difference in someone else's life.

Another, perhaps unexpected, joy is that when we focus less on our own needs and more on the needs of others, we find God working in our lives so that our own needs are miraculously met and exceeded. Developing a life of generosity inevitably means that we become better stewards of what God has provided.

Additional Resources You May Find Helpful

- *Shift 2.0,* by Phil Maynard (available at the Excellence in Ministry Coaching website at emc3coaching.com, as well as marketsquarebooks.com and cokesbury.com)

- *Discipler: An Interactive Guide to Intentional, Relational, and Accountable Discipleship,* by Phil Maynard and Eddie Pipkin (available at marketsquarebooks.com and cokesbury.com)

- *Financial Peace University,* by Dave Ramsey

- *Enough,* by Adam Hamilton

Recap of a Life of Generosity

Living a life of generosity means that we are faithful stewards of all that God has provided for us so that we may be expressions of God's love through the responsible use of our time, energy, and financial resources.

Supporting Scripture:

> **"If you are faithful in little things, you will be faithful in large ones. But if you are dishonest in little things, you won't be honest with greater responsibilities"**
>
> **Luke 16:10**

Jesus sat down opposite the place where the offerings were put and watched the crowd putting their money into the temple treasury. Many rich people threw in large amounts. But a poor widow came and put in two very small copper coins, worth only a few cents. Calling his disciples to him, Jesus said, "Truly I tell you, this poor widow has put more into the treasury than all the others. They all gave out of their wealth; but she, out of her poverty, put in everything — all she had to live on."

Mark 12:41-44

Behaviors reflecting a life of generosity:

- Giving proportionately to the ministries of the church and parachurch service organizations and moving toward a tithe and beyond.

- Responding to needs that God places in our path.

- Helping someone in need each week.

Questions for Reflection and Discussion

1. How do you see the use of financial resources as a spiritual practice?

2. In Philippians 4:12, the Apostle Paul writes that he has learned the secret of being content. What is that secret? How have you used that wisdom to guide your own life?

3. How do you demonstrate compassion through a life of generosity?

4. The ancient Hebrew people were instructed to not reap the edges or gather the gleanings of their crops (Leviticus 19). How is that teaching relevant to our lives today?

5. What is a tithe? The tithe is described as just the right amount to give to the ministry of the church or service organizations. Why?

6. What are the three rules John Wesley suggested for the use of financial resources? How do these apply to your life?

7. What practice might you be willing to commit to this week in order to grow in a life of generosity?

CHAPTER SIX

Growing Disciples

Most local churches and even whole denominations have some form of mission statement that refers to the church existing for the purpose of "making disciples." For example, in the United Methodist tradition (our denominational home base), the purpose of the Church is stated clearly and unequivocally:

> To make disciples of Jesus Christ for the transformation of the world. [1]

This is appropriate since Jesus [himself] issued the call commonly known as The Great Commission: "Go, therefore, and make disciples. . ." (Matthew 28:19).

If we are part of a local church or a denomination (especially leadership of either), these are relevant questions:

- Over the past few decades, how has the Church lived into this calling to make disciples?

- How successful has the Church been in creating transformed lives? Specifically, lives that reflect the life of Jesus?

- How did Jesus show us the way by demonstrating the fulfillment of the Great Commission during his own ministry here on Earth?

- What might we learn from how Jesus himself made disciples? And how might that impact the way we do ministry?

Current Reality

Despite the significant investment of time, financial resources, and amazing educational options over the past few decades, research indicates that the Church is not doing all that well at creating transformed lives. The Church is struggling to produce disciples who behave like Jesus. Researcher George Barna analyzed the data in his book, *Growing True Disciples.* He found little to no statistical difference between the way 'born again believers' and 'non-believers' conduct themselves. [2]

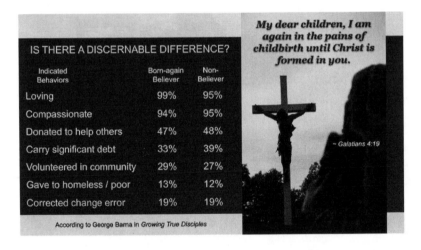

IS THERE A DISCERNABLE DIFFERENCE?		
Indicated Behaviors	Born-again Believer	Non-Believer
Loving	99%	95%
Compassionate	94%	95%
Donated to help others	47%	48%
Carry significant debt	33%	39%
Volunteered in community	29%	27%
Gave to homeless / poor	13%	12%
Corrected change error	19%	19%

According to George Barna in *Growing True Disciples*

My dear children, I am again in the pains of childbirth until Christ is formed in you.

~ Galatians 4:19

Apparently, our highly developed spiritual formation strategies have not been making much of a difference when it comes to real-world behaviors.

So, what have we been doing?

For decades, the Church, in keeping with the understanding

of disciples being learners and following the cultural approach of classroom learning experiences, has approached discipleship as a programmatic ministry. At the local level, we group the congregation by age-level categories and provide age-appropriate educational experiences, often based around an academic calendar year that mimics the school calendar.

Whenever we at Excellence in Ministry Coaching work with congregations to establish an intentional discipleship pathway, we start by asking what they already have in place. Nine times out of ten, someone proudly presents a flyer or brochure that describes the classes that are being offered each semester of the coming year.

There is, of course, nothing wrong with offering classes. It is good for people to learn about God and Jesus and the Church and theology and the many related topics. It's just not sufficient to only *learn* about them. This isn't discipleship. It's Christian Education, and while Christian Education serves a noble and valuable purpose, this approach to individual spiritual development isn't creating disciples who live like Jesus.

Discipleship isn't just about information. It's about transformation.

Discipleship isn't just about knowledge. It's about behaviors.

In addition to adding insight into what isn't working, research like Barna's has also helped the Church understand what people's own perceptions are about what they need in order to grow as disciples. It turns out that people are surprisingly thoughtful and self-aware about their own needs. Topping the list from the research study, "Reveal," done by Willow Creek Community Church, which surveyed folks from 1,000 churches, respondents identified these needs:

- Help understanding the Bible (teaching them how to study/ exegete the Scriptures and apply lessons to life).

- Help growing in a personal relationship with Christ.

- The challenge to take responsibility for their own spiritual growth.

- Leaders who model and consistently reinforce how to grow spiritually. [3]

Those needs could be challenging to address in our typical classroom setting. It doesn't mean it's not possible with the right curriculum and an excellent leader, but the traditional design of such educational offerings works against many of the desired dynamics identified by the survey. Our cookie-cutter approach of offering "Five Essential Practices for the Christian Life" or "Ten Steps to Personal Holiness" isn't cutting it.

In the context of a classroom setting, for example, it's more difficult to move beyond general tools for understanding the Scriptures and help someone see how what is being revealed might apply directly to their life, taking time to consider the details of their unique life conditions. What helps one person develop an awareness of Christ may not work as well for someone else. What helps another person grow their relationship with God might not work for the first person. When attending a worship service, a person may hear a sermon that ends with a dramatic challenge to take a next step in their spiritual journey, but what that next step may look like will vary greatly across the needs of a given congregation. If 200 people hear the challenge delivered in that sermon, there are likely at least 175 varieties of response. Who helps the individual disciple figure out appropriate next steps? Who models what it means for a follower of Jesus — newbie or old hand — to continue to grow spiritually?

Some congregations have discovered that the typical six-week classroom-style small group is not producing disciples who are experiencing life transformation. They have moved to a longer-term approach, often called Life Groups, where deeper relationships are the goal, and disciples have more opportunity to challenge, encourage, and speak into one another's lives. This is a step in the right direction. The challenge with this approach, however, is to be intentional about providing great spiritual formation content and to equip leaders to meet the needs of instruction, mentoring, coaching, and accountable discipleship.

So, if the current models are struggling (either in concept or execution), and if what we have been doing has been less than successful in helping people actually become like Jesus, where can we turn for a better way?

We suggest doing what Jesus did.

Challenges to Discipleship
(in Jesus' day and ours)

Lack of Vision

Stephen Covey, in *The 7 Habits of Highly Successful People,* starts with this organizing idea:

Begin with the end in mind. [4]

Covey's directive applies to the realm of discipleship. It is hard to get people to commit to a process of personal/spiritual development if they cannot see the end goal. Much of the preceding material in this book was about casting a vision for discipleship, the Kingdom life to which we are called. The specific behaviors we considered were keys to the formation of a heart that automatically acts with the attitude of Jesus — the "life ofs" we spent the last few chapters exploring.

Much of the teaching and preaching of Jesus was focused on casting a vision for this Kingdom life that he modeled. He challenged people's perspectives, some long-held assumptions, and many religious practices, saying, "You have heard . . . but I say to you." This is what preachers do in worship messages as they invite us to see and engage the world from a Kingdom perspective. This is what teachers, mentors, apprentices, and coaches do as they model, question, encourage, and support the development of disciples in the Kingdom life.

If we are to engage people in a journey toward discipleship, toward becoming more like Jesus, we must help them see a picture of what that life could look like for them.

Contentment

In a Western world culture in which we have routinely sepa-
rated the idea of being a Christian from expectations about
becoming more like Jesus, we are hamstrung by our desire to
maintain our cocoon of contentment. We like life as it is. Why
change? Why endanger our comfort and safety by committing to
becoming something more?

Note to pastors and church leaders: It's tempting to be judgmental about people who are wrapped up in their own contentment with how things are in their relationship with God and
the Church (or lack thereof). Resist that judgmental urge. We,
the leaders of the Church, have been complicit in the creation
of this mindset. We have exchanged Jesus' vision for authentic
discipleship with an obsessive focus on worship service attendance and budgets. If we have any sustained focus on spiritual
development, it is usually limited to reading the Bible and
praying as vaguely established goals. We are as responsible
as the bogeyman of 'culture' for the tenuity of the discipleship
commitment.

This lack of discipleship enthusiasm is not a new development. As we noted at the very beginning of this book, even
Jesus had people turn away because of his "hard teaching."
They got cold feet when Jesus reached the part of the sermon
where it was clear that an expectation of behavioral change
was going to be part of the package. To help people move beyond
this natural reluctance, we must use the same strategy that
Jesus used (and the same strategy that works for promoting
transformative change in any organization). We create a sense
of urgency. In the case of discipleship, we help people see the
amazing benefits for both their lives and the Kingdom impact.

137

Inward Focus

Much of the Church's focus on discipleship has traditionally come in the form of getting 'saved' and being obedient to a couple of key spiritual practices (e.g. Bible study and prayer). While these elements are a portion of what discipleship is all about, they fall short of representing its entirety. In fact, growth as a disciple necessarily moves a person away from a focus on oneself and toward a focus on those outside the faith community. This movement is represented in each of the "life of" continuums presented in graphic form in previous chapters.

For example, in the "Life of Hospitality" chapter, when we look at the continuum graphic, the discipleship journey begins with feeling accepted (which is all about us), but arrives at a state of maturity that is focused on helping others discover God's love (which is all about them).

A LIFE OF HOSPITALITY			
I am curiously drawn to the Christians who graciously accept me as if I belong with them already.	I am called not only to receive, but also to offer God's gracious acceptance to others.	I seek to relate to others both in the church and beyond in ways that reflect God's hospitality to me.	I intentionally seek to build relationships with unchurched people in order to share God's love.

In the "Life of Worship" chapter, discipleship begins with having our needs met (which is all about us), but we reach maturity by living as a witness to bring honor and glory to God (which is all about others).

A LIFE OF WORSHIP			
I attend worship when a friend invites me, when it is convenient, or when I feel a need.	I attend worship regularly, but I am growing to realize that I must attend to God every day.	I attend worship regularly and set aside time daily for personal worship.	I honor God in the ways that I work, play, and engage others in relationships.

138

Disciples become focused on the transformation of the world as they move toward maturity. This is a shift in focus from selfish desires and parochial motivations to a Jesus-oriented focus, which takes in a far wider community of concerns.

Commitment

As well-intentioned as people may be when they start along the pathway of discipleship, the reality is that life gets in the way. It's difficult to maintain the discipling process as a priority, whether working in a small group setting or a one-to-one accountability partnership. People don't follow through. They miss and reschedule appointments. They get distracted by things that seem more pressing. This is normal. This is life. It doesn't mean the person is a failure. It doesn't mean the leader is a failure, or the accountability partner is a failure. It's just an affirmation of the truth that we all need some patience and structure.

Linear View and Expectations

A friend of Phil's wrote a book titled *The Meandering Way.* It's about the spiritual journey and how that spiritual journey is anything but linear. People get discouraged and want to give up when they take three steps forward and then find themselves falling two steps back. But it turns out such halting progress is normal. It is also true that there is often no immediate and automatic cause and effect in play when we initiate spiritual practices. Just because we start having a time of prayer does not mean we will automatically find ourselves with a "direct line to God." These things take time.

If a person is in the discipler role (the senior partner), they will need to be patient, encouraging, and respectful of these struggles in the person they are guiding. If a person is being discipled (the junior partner), they will need those same qualities, perhaps oriented in a different direction: patience and respect toward their more mature partner, as well as patience with themselves. We'll have plenty of practice in both of these roles, because at every stage of our lifelong spiritual journey, if we're serious about it, we'll find ourselves discipling somebody even as we are simultaneously being discipled by someone else. We should always be teacher and learner. A ladder of relationships is necessary, and we all inhabit different rungs in different seasons. And on every rung we'll need patience.

Characteristics of Good Discipling Relationships

Relational

Discipleship happens in relationships. It's a 'contact sport.' When we want to help someone grow as a disciple, our first impulse should not be to give them a book or training guide (although these may be helpful resources) and send them off to a corner to process what they're reading. We get them into a relationship with someone who is further along the path of discipleship.

This discipler (partner) walks alongside the disciple. When the junior partner doesn't understand something, the discipler explains it. When they stumble, the discipler helps them up and dusts them off. When they start off on a 'rabbit trail,' the discipler brings them back to focus. When they need a helping hand, the discipler reaches out. When they experience success, the discipler celebrates with them and for them!

Consider these words of the Apostle Paul:

> For you know that we dealt with each of you as a father deals with his own children, encouraging, comforting and urging you to live lives worthy of God, who calls you into his Kingdom and glory.
>
> **1 Thessalonians 2:11-12**

Discipleship is relational.

Focused

If we are to proceed according to Stephen Covey's call to "begin with the end in mind," before we can partner with someone to help them get somewhere, we must be clear about our destination.

Good disciplers help people see the end-goal of the process (becoming like Jesus). They help the disciple keep their eyes on the target. In Matthew 14, Peter gets out of the boat and walks on the water toward Jesus. Everything goes great until he gets distracted by the wind and waves. When he takes his eyes off Jesus, he begins to sink. In the same way, the disciple must keep their eyes on Jesus. A disciple must stay focused to become like Jesus.

Intentional

If we are in pursuit of a clear goal, it just makes sense to do specific things that will support movement toward that goal. This is intentional discipleship. It may be a great thing to have disciples engage in the newest 'talking head' video study of the Bible (with lots of available choices for your favorite popular preacher/teacher of the moment). But, if the goal is to encourage a specific waypoint — say, a life of generosity, as an example — perhaps the training should be intentionally focused on biblical financial management. If the goal is developing a growing awareness of the presence of God, perhaps the training should introduce the breadth of spiritual practices that help develop this awareness. You get the idea. This is not to say that we shouldn't use 'talking head' video series, just that we should be intentional about how we guide people toward their goals.

Developmental

Discipleship is about growth. It's about movement toward something (an important distinction since, after all, even 'backsliding' is a form of movement). In the previous section, we presented this growth as a continuum of behaviors that reflect a trajectory of development. This developmental aspect is not limited to behaviors which are considered official 'spiritual practices.' We cannot separate our spiritual lives from our physical lives or our emotional lives. Jesus emphasized this in the Great Commandment, which he said summaries all the teaching and the law:

> **"Love the Lord your God with all of your heart, soul, mind, and strength."**
>
> **Matthew 22:37**

Good discipleship is holistic. It is about developing our entire being.

Accountable

Good discipleship includes an element of accountability. Jesus didn't just tell them how Kingdom life was done or even just demonstrate how Kingdom life was done. He held the twelve disciples accountable for developing a Kingdom perspective and practices. However, remembering that we are not Jesus, this role of holding folks accountable has practical limitations. The discipler is not the disciple's mother, supervisor, or boss. The discipler is the disciple's partner. The disciple is not accountable to the discipler as an individual. They are ultimately accountable to God and to themselves.

To the extent that we enter into accountability partnerships with anyone (discipler, disciple, mentor, coach, or small group partners), it is a voluntary, free will, noncompulsory relationship. It is fed by honesty, trust, compassion, and love. We may ask an accountability partner how something is working, what they are learning, where they are in the process, all of which are ways of providing accountability. But they are accountable to God and to themselves. We are not issuing grades. We are not giving final exams.

Poorly executed accountability arrangements have destroyed many discipling relationships. Accountability is important, but it must be structured wholesomely and humbly. Expectations are important, because people aspire to live into expectations. Expectations, however, must always be anchored in love, because love is not a shackle. Love is a bridge.

How Jesus Made Disciples

Some General Observations

Before we dive too deeply into the specifics about how Jesus engaged people to help them grow as disciples, let's do an observational flyover.

First, Jesus was a great teacher and often drew crowds that even our best and brightest preachers can only dream about.

The people in these crowds were said to be amazed at his teaching. And rightly so. Jesus was the smartest man on Earth. Plus, he performed miracles.

Jesus was casting an extraordinary vision of God's Kingdom. In a religious culture that had relegated Kingdom life to a massive collection of rules and interpretations, Jesus proclaimed a way of life where God could be joyfully celebrated and intimately experienced. To a religious establishment that had put God in a box (quite literally, by way of the Holy of Holies), Jesus proclaimed a God available to the people, all the people, even the people the religious establishment had shut out.

The multitudes who followed Jesus around the hillsides were not disciples of Jesus in the sense of *becoming* like Jesus. They were fans of Jesus. They liked the idea of being taken care of (healed and fed) and of Jesus demonstrating miraculous power (walking on water, turning water into wine). They were amazed, intrigued, challenged, chastised, and even comforted at times. But they were not yet committed to a new way of living. Jesus proclaimed the Good News, introduced the Kingdom at hand, and related his teachings to everyday life that the people could grasp. Jesus helped people catch a glimpse of the life God intended. That Good News vision needs to be fleshed out in more intimate and accountable settings.

This in no way discounts the impact of the preaching and teaching components that dominate our contemporary worship gatherings. These preaching and teaching times are opportunities to invite people to consider next steps in their discipleship journey and respond to the promptings of the Holy Spirit.

However, for many local churches, the focus of preaching and teaching, as well as the songs we sing and the liturgy we share, is the casting of a Kingdom vision. The nuts and bolts

144

of discipleship, especially accountability, most often happen in smaller contexts.

Second, Jesus demonstrated this truth by pouring himself into a small group of people. While Jesus proclaimed the Kingdom of God to vast crowds, he gathered a small group of men and women around him to disciple in the tradition of the rabbis of his day. It was this group that would be equipped by him to "turn the world upside down" as was said of them in Acts 17. They lived and traveled with Jesus. They received his instruction. They tried and failed and then tried again to do the things he did. They began to understand a Kingdom that would find its fullness in servanthood and grace. And they were sent directly to do the work Jesus had begun.

It is interesting to note that while Jesus gathered the twelve disciples to do life together as a team, he also engaged even more deeply with a group of three — an inner circle if you will. Peter, James, and John are mentioned multiple times as a distinct subset within the original twelve disciples. Michael Hyatt describes how this breakout group fits within the leadership strategy of Jesus:

> Jesus had an inner circle comprised of Peter, James, and John. He took them on special outings (see Matthew 17:1). He allowed them to witness his greatest glory (see Mark 9:2–3) and his deepest temptations (see Mark 14:33–34).
>
> He prayed with them (see Luke 9:28). He taught them things He did not teach the others (see Matthew 17:2; Mark 5:37–43). He even introduced them to His heavenly family (see Matthew 17:3). They were his closest friends and confidants. [5]

Greg Ogden, writing in his book *Transforming Discipleship,* again draws on this image of three (a discipleship triad) as a uniquely strong approach for transformational discipleship:

The person leading a discipling triad need not hold a position of authority, except to be the keeper of the covenant . . . influence will naturally occur within the relationship. The depth of one's spiritual life, and insight, the evident passion to serve Christ, the application of Scripture to life, will all naturally flow out in the dynamic interchange . . . there is an environment for transformation. [6]

When we think about discipleship in the church, it is often in the Paul-Timothy model (where a mature disciple partners with a novice) or in a programmatic approach to small group ministries. In many smaller congregations, the idea of creating small group ministries is daunting. But what if, instead, we were to focus on encouraging this model of triads to provide teaching, intimacy, discipling, and accountability? It was, after all, modeled by Jesus.

Third, Jesus welcomed people from all walks of life. From tax collectors to sinners, lepers to Sadducees, the infirm to prostitutes, Jesus engaged people who were different and often considered unacceptable. The Gospel message is not just for the righteous. As Jesus put it, "I have not come to call the righteous, but sinners" (Mark 2:17).

Fourth, Jesus engaged people of all ages. We love the heart of Jesus as he tells his disciples, "Let the little children come to me and do not hinder them, for the Kingdom of heaven belongs to such as these" (Matthew 19:14). Jesus' ministry was intergenerational. The children were intermixed in the multitudes and in the direct ministry of Jesus so that they might learn from him. Consider this in contrast to our programmatic approach of age-level ministry, as Johanna Myers notes in an article titled "Are You Teaching People about Faith? Or How to Practice It?":

146

If our whole approach to disciple making is about educating people, age-level ministry becomes incredibly important because teaching a five-year-old is different than teaching a ten-year-old, a youth, or a young adult. But if the focus is on developing practices, it is important to learn from people who are skilled in the practices of faith. And interspersing the generations makes more sense than having everyone broken down into age-level ministry groupings. [7]

Fifth, Jesus tied his teaching to real life. From the planting of seeds that would bring a great harvest, to the hauls of great fish in the nets of the disciples, to the comparison of the Kingdom to the leaven in bread, Jesus spoke in the language of the people and used examples to which they could relate. The stories he told most were generated by his bond with the people and the everyday life they experienced.

Sixth, Jesus met people where they were on their journey to God. It is abundantly clear that Jesus did not expect people to be 'cleaned up' before they could participate in the Kingdom reality. He met them where they were, and he led them towards where he wanted them to be (sometimes gently and sometimes by offering a shock to their system). To the woman caught in the act of adultery, he says, "Go and sin no more" (John 8:11). To the expert in the law in the story of the Good Samaritan, Jesus says, "Now go and do the same" (Luke 10:37).

Seventh, Jesus was a servant leader. Everything Jesus did was for the people God loves. There was no gain, no prestige, no power to be gained from the people who were the focus of his ministry. He paid the ultimate price of selfless servanthood by laying down his life for his friends.

Eighth, Jesus was a multiplier. He modeled a significant mathematical truth about how disciples are made. Even though being fully God, Jesus took on our humanity and as Eugene

Peterson puts it in *The Message,* "He moved into the neighborhood" (John 1:14). He chose to transform the world by engaging the world one-on-one. Jesus multiplied his discipling impact by making disciples who made disciples. Jesus sent them out to witness to the Kingdom at hand and do the ministry he had modeled. Following his death, those disciples literally turned the world on its head as they, in turn, made disciples across the map.

These general observations about the way Jesus made disciples invite us to consider the techniques we might employ to help people become stronger disciples. One cannot miss the intimate nature of Jesus' connection with those he discipled. The big group gatherings were focused on vision-casting. The equipping of disciples was very personal. It still is.

With this framework of observations in mind, let's turn to some specific methods Jesus used to communicate the Kingdom life in order to move the disciples more fully in the direction of that life. How might we apply his methodology in our quest to transform the world?

Questions for Reflection and Discussion

1. We identify four obstacles to growth as a disciple of Jesus. What have you found to be a struggle in your own development or a struggle in helping others grow?

2. Who has been a partner with you in your growth as a disciple? What have they done that was most helpful?

3. How have you experienced accountability for your growth as a disciple? How did this support your development?

4. Jesus had an inner circle (a triad of three disciples) for whom he provided deeper exploration of the Kingdom life. What has been your experience with having a couple of close friends to journey with you?

5. What opportunity have you taken to partner with someone from a different age group to help them grow as a disciple? What have you learned from the experience?

6. How are you multiplying yourself as a disciple of Jesus? We are given the imperative to "go, therefore, and make disciples." How are you living out this imperative?

CHAPTER SEVEN

Discipling Relationships and Skills

Modeling the Kingdom Life

Jesus is the ultimate example of practicing what you preach. There is no gap between what he said and what he did. The people were amazed at his empathy, his teaching, his witness, and his miracles. What you saw was what you got with Jesus.

We are not Jesus, and neither are you. Neither are those we might have the opportunity to disciple ("to disciple" being the active process of helping someone else along in their journey to become more like Jesus). God calls us to be ourselves, fully ourselves, as we were lovingly created to be. Nobody expects us to be Jesus, just to dedicate ourselves to becoming more like Jesus, to develop the kind of life that Jesus modeled. If we are to help others on this journey, it is good to keep this adage in mind: "You can't give what you don't have."

In every way you can think of, Jesus modeled the Kingdom life: from welcoming all, even the most unlikely, to bringing healing to those isolated from their communities by disease, to taking time to enjoy his deep relationships with his friends, to finding time alone with God, and even to challenging people to discover a new way of being. These were the revolutionary statements and actions that drew people to Jesus — then and now.

This is true whether applied to people within the church — those who come through the church doors actively seeking to be inspired by Jesus' message — or those outside the church, who may not be actively professing admiration of Jesus and his people, but are directly influenced by the words and witness of those of us who claim to be acting as conduits of God's grace. They are looking closely to see how we model that life. Unfortunately, the general consensus is that we appear to be falling short. Take Mahatma Gandhi, considered to be one of the most enlightened humans in history, who quipped: "I like your Christ. I do not like your Christians. Your Christians are so unlike your Christ." [1]

In a large survey about attitudes towards religion called the "Fermi Project," discussed in depth in the book *UnChristian,* Gabe Lyons highlights the perspective of 16- to- 29-year-olds, related to the Church. [2]

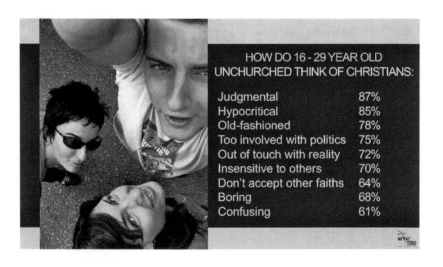

HOW DO 16 - 29 YEAR OLD UNCHURCHED THINK OF CHRISTIANS:	
Judgmental	87%
Hypocritical	85%
Old-fashioned	78%
Too involved with politics	75%
Out of touch with reality	72%
Insensitive to others	70%
Don't accept other faiths	64%
Boring	68%
Confusing	61%

It's not a pretty picture.

You don't have to be an "outsider" to wish the church would better honor its mission and upgrade its methods. In the research done by Chicago's Willow Creek Community Church, here are the top five things that active church members crave. [3]

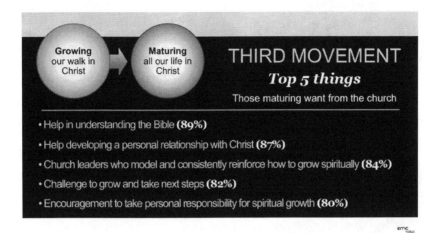

In the opening chapters of this book, we identified three dimensions of spiritual growth (belonging to the body of Christ, becoming more like Jesus, and blessing the world). When we ask people about ways the Church can support their spiritual growth, we hear a familiar refrain for a longing for a demonstration of leadership that applies equally in all three categories: people long for "church leaders who model and consistently reinforce how to grow spiritually." People need church leaders who demonstrate what it's like to belong to the body of Christ, become more like Jesus, and bless the world — not just through talking about these topics, or managing meetings about these topics, but by visibly living out these principles.

It is important to emphasize at this point that each of us, no matter our status within the "church food chain," can and should be a leader in the sense of modeling good leadership skills wherever we have influence.

Leadership is a process of social influence, which maximizes the efforts of others toward the achievement of a goal:

- Leadership stems from social influence, not authority or power.

- Leadership requires others, and that implies they don't need to be 'direct reports.'

- No mention of personality traits, attributes, or even a title; there are many styles, many paths, to effective leadership.

- It includes a goal, not influence with no intended outcome.[4]

Modeling draws upon the age-old understanding of human behavior that the American psychologist Albert Bandura terms "observational learning":

> [This is a method] of learning that consists of observing and modeling another individual's behavior, attitudes, or emotional expressions . . . four conditions were necessary.

- **Attention:** If an organism is going to learn anything from a model, he or she must be paying attention to it and the behavior it exhibits.

- **Retention:** Being able to remember the behavior that was witnessed.

- **Reproduction:** The physical and mental ability of the individual to copy the behavior he or she observed.

- **Motivation:** The most important aspect. If the human or animal does not have a reason for imitating the behavior, then no amount of attention, retention, or reproduction will overcome the lack of motivation.[5]

One of the key benchmarks for maturity as a disciple is that we are actively discipling someone else. This may be the most significant form of leadership we ever provide. And modeling the behaviors we are hoping to promote in someone else is a key form of this leadership.

Imagine the possibilities for employing this modeling approach:

- Spiritual friends learning from each other as they journey together toward maturing discipleship.

- Intergenerational impact, as some of our more mature disciples partner with someone from the generation above or below them to model a particular behavioral set. This, by the way, is not always from older to younger. Some of our more senior adults could learn a great deal from the younger generation.

- Small group leaders providing modeling behaviors like the practice of spiritual disciplines, pastoral care, worship, hospitality, generosity, and service.

- A strengthening of relational evangelism as we model for our friends, neighbors, and co-workers what a Kingdom lifestyle looks like.

- Encouragement for the children in our families as we help them develop practices that will serve them as lifelong maturing disciples.

Small Groups

Jesus is well-known for his deep connection to a small group of dedicated followers: The Twelve. In fact, most who teach about small group ministries define small groups as being between three and twelve participants. Jesus certainly did ministry with larger groups, as evidenced by the many stories from the Gospels of his work with houses full, synagogues full, and even entire hillsides and beachsides full of followers. But Jesus also poured himself into a small group that would have an outsized, historic impact.

Dave Ferguson and Warren Bird, in *Hero Maker,* analyze this simple but profound strategy:

> In John 3:22, the Bible makes an easily overlooked, seemingly mundane statement: "Jesus and his disciples went out into the Judean countryside, where he spent some time with them."
>
> What Jesus did is really quite simple. He selected just a few people — he focused on twelve — and they hung out with him and did ministry alongside him. Yet when Jesus spent some time with these twelve apprentices, something big happened. The word for spend time in Greek is pronounced dia-tree-bo (and transliterated diatribe). *Dia* means *against,* and *tribo* means *to rub.* So diatribe literally means *to rub against* **or** *to rub off.* It literally means *to spend time together rubbing off on each other.* [6]

While twelve seems to be a magic number for a variety of reasons — including the fact that Jesus had twelve disciples — of even more significance is what it meant to be part of his small group. This is the real gift Jesus gave us for partnering in small groups for discipleship:

- The disciples did life together. The small group of Jesus followers didn't gather for six weeks to study a particular topic or book of the Bible. They lived together and traveled together and learned together and ate together and served together.

- The disciples developed deep relationships. They spent much time together building a level of trust in one another. This level of trust allowed them to question and challenge and support and encourage and even rebuke one another. That depth of relationship doesn't happen in a short-term course.

- The disciples learned together. While the actual mechanics of the teaching and learning will be explored more deeply in the next section, it is important to note that the disciples experienced a discernible growth in their understanding about what the Kingdom life was all about, and this growth was sparked by the direct teaching of Jesus and their experiences together.

- The disciples prayed and worshiped together. From the request, "Lord, teach us how to pray" to the participation in the religious feasts to the gathering at the Seder Meal for the Last Supper, the disciples engaged as a brotherhood in worship and spiritual practices.

- The disciples served together. Wherever Jesus and his disciples went, they served the people they encountered. They fed the multitudes, healed the sick, raised the dead, cast out demons, and cured the physically challenged. Their discipleship had an external focus. It wasn't just about them and their own internal development.

- The disciples were accountable. Jesus frequently checked on the progress of his disciples by asking questions like, "Who do you say that I am?" or "Do you also want to leave?" In Luke 10, for instance, the disciples, who had been sent out in a great witnessing campaign to cure the sick and proclaim the Kingdom in their midst, returned to give a detailed accounting of their progress.

Since Jesus chose this small group discipleship model, it's a good sign that it's an effective strategy for us to use as well. Check out the way you can connect the small group model to the "dimensions of being" discipleship model we've highlighted throughout this book. We'll call this the "3-B" approach to small groups:

- A small group commits to BELONGING to the body of Christ.

- A small group commits to BECOMING more like Jesus.

- A small group commits to BLESSING the world.

To be counted as a 3-B small group, that group commits to each of the B's. Each meeting is framed around the 3-B's:

- For the belonging to the body of Christ element, groups are encouraged to have a time of worship, prayer, and fellowship (including catch-up time and refreshments).

- For the becoming more like Jesus element, groups are asked to provide some type of teaching component (Bible study, spiritual practices, etc.) and to hold one another accountable for how this learning is applied to real life. While each group is asked to engage some specific themes for intentional development, beyond those themes, each group selects topics and resources that meet needs of the group members or are of common interest.

- For the blessing the world element, groups are expected to serve outside the church in the community in some way every four to six weeks. This is done as a group experience so it will be less intimidating for individuals and create stronger bonds between the members of the group. Groups are encouraged to process the experience following the time of service, considering what it was like to give of themselves in that way, how those being served were blessed, how members of the group were blessed in return, and where they saw God in the midst of serving.

That's just one of many effective options for organizing small groups, and, of course, this whole idea of what we now call "small group ministry" is nothing new under the sun.

These are just new iterations of a basic model that has served humanity well for generations.

A few years ago, Phil was driving author Eric Geiger to the airport after a workshop based on Eric's book, *Simple Church*. As they drove along and unpacked how the session had gone, he turned to Phil at one point and asked, "What's wrong with you people?"

Phil's response was, "You're going to have to be more specific."

Geiger said, "Everywhere I go, in every tribe of Christianity I work with, they are using John Wesley's Class Meeting approach to discipleship. Everybody except for your tribe [the Methodists]. What's wrong with you people?"

Geiger had caught on to the distinctions related to the Wesleyan Class Meeting approach that set the standard for how to do small groups. Wesley's Classes were small, usually around twelve persons. There was a class leader, who basically served as a mentor for the members of the class. The focus was on behaviors and the development of spiritual practices. Each member of the group was accountable for how they were living into those behaviors, and the group served to support the development of each member as a growing/maturing disciple.

This, of course sounds, sounds a lot like an update of things Jesus did.

Teaching

Teaching has become the default role for the Church in partnering with people to help them grow as disciples. There are reasons this is true:

- **Cultural Expectations:** In our modern society, education has become the 'go to' approach for helping people grow in

159

any dimension of life. If you want someone to develop skills in graphic design, you send them to graphic design school. If you want someone to learn how to pray, you send them to a class on prayer. If you want someone to learn to share the Gospel, you send them to seminary.

According to research, the efficacy of this approach is somewhere between 20-40%. This means that, in terms of real-life application or transformation, we hit the mark less than half of the time. [7]

- **Sense of Accomplishment:** Presenting reams of detailed information is the easiest approach to take if we want to *feel like* we're making disciples. It creates a sense that we are actively doing something significant. We can organize the content and give supporting references and even real-life examples. This doesn't necessarily accomplish the goal of transformed lives. This doesn't mean the students are held accountable for converting learning to action. The problem is that it's too easy to divorce informational content from lived experience and practical application.

Jesus takes a different approach.

Jesus used direct instruction, coupled with practical application. The disciples came to him and said, "Lord, teach us how to pray." Jesus does not respond with a dissertation on the history and cultural significance of prayer. Nor does he form a committee that is then designated to form a plan to explore the best ways to teach prayer. Jesus teaches them how to pray, right there on the spot. He gives them a practical model for prayer so good that we still use it every Sunday: it's called the Lord's Prayer.

Jesus used examples from everyday life to communicate many Kingdom truths:

- The parable of the sower

- Yeast to leaven bread

- The lost coin

- The widow's mite

- Ritual washing

Jesus demonstrated how to heal diseases and cure physical limitations. Then he invited the disciples to try it themselves. Jesus practiced a model of field education where he sent the disciples out to proclaim the Good News and heal the sick. Then he processed their experiences with them when they returned.

Bob Logan and Charles Ridley, in *The Discipleship Difference,* summarize it this way:

Jesus used the world as his workshop for making disciples. He brought his disciples outside, into the real world, and gave them practical, hands-on experience. He didn't do a seminar on casting out demons; he had his disciples try it and then helped them figure out how to get it right. We learn how to swim in the same way — in a pool, not in a classroom. Although classes in swimming technique can be supplemental and helpful, there's no substitute for getting in the water and trying it.

Our character is shaped by facing real-life challenges that move us outside of our comfort zones.[8]

Teaching has an important role in the quest to help disciples become more like Jesus. However, teaching is not a stand-alone strategy that can get them to that goal without the other companion approaches we have discussed. If transformative change is to happen, we have to be doing more than just providing information. The information (content) is valuable. It is part of the discipleship process. But it can't be the totality of the process.

Mentoring

Mentoring is a word that is often used interchangeably with terms like *coaching* and *apprenticing.* In the professional coaching world, we make a much clearer distinction between these forms of partnering with someone for their personal/faith/discipleship/professional development. There is consensus that the terms *mentoring* and *apprenticing* are very closely related, while *coaching* is seen to be a very different tool for personal development.

Jeremie Kubicek makes the following distinction between mentoring and apprenticing:

> Mentoring is controlled by the mentee. Typically, mentees approach mentors for guidance in an area they want help. Mentees establish the topic and desired outcome.

> Apprenticeship begins with mentors not mentees. You approach them saying something like, "I see an area in your life that is holding you back. I believe I can help." If you have leadership skills, habits, attitudes, or behaviors that help you succeed, apprenticing means you pour what you have into another. [9]

Darryl Wilson, carries the discussion of this distinction further:

> *Mentoring* is focused upon helping an individual Christian grow from believer to follower to disciple to discipler. . . . To

summarize, mentoring is a one-on-one relationship designed to help the Christian to grow in Christ.

Apprenticing is focused upon intentional leadership multiplication. Usually this is done best one-on-one. The apprenticing leader is seeking to accomplish one of two tasks: (a) replace himself/herself as a leader in order to move on to new challenges or (b) train a new individual in a similar area of responsibility. [10]

One of our favorite descriptions of mentoring comes from the master coach, Val Hastings, in his Accelerated Coach Training resource:

Mentoring is a process of guiding another along a path that you (the mentor) have already traveled. The sharing or guidance includes experiences and learning from the mentor's own experience. The underlying premise is that the insight and guidance of the mentor can accelerate the learning curve of the one being mentored. [11]

Mentoring is best understood as a partnership between someone with some expertise and experience in something and someone who is seeking to develop expertise. It is a pouring into a person by the mentor, drawing on the mentor's training, experience, and character. The mentor does not have to be an expert in a given topic, just further down the path toward expertise. With the definition of "pouring oneself into another person" as the central metaphor, Jesus perfectly fits the bill for the title of ultimate mentor.

One of the most common uses of mentors in the local church is that of creating sponsors to partner with newcomers to the congregational life. These sponsors (mentors by another name) model what it means to be an engaged participant in the life of the church. They invite newcomers to explore how they might become connected in ways that are both a blessing to themselves and to the church.

The role of mentors has received a more programmatic approach in the last decade through the Radical Mentoring process created by Andy Stanley's North Point Ministries. Radical Mentoring is a men's ministry focus built on mentoring concepts and designed to develop leaders. The mentors are selected for their spiritual maturity, and each mentor partners with a small group of younger men (mentees) with whom they will work for nine months. They read and discuss specified books focused on spiritual development, have assigned homework, but most of all do life together. The mentor, through listening and sharing in deep spiritual conversations, has the opportunity to pour himself into the lives of the mentees.

In the business world, mentors are a support to employees with great potential to help them develop necessary skills, process situations, develop networks, and reach greater levels of success in their careers. In the church world, mentors can help people do all those things, too, but their true and sacred purpose is to help people become more like Jesus. Sometimes this includes a specified curriculum (as in the Radical Mentoring program of North Point Ministries). Sometimes it is just a commitment to meet regularly and talk about how God is speaking into someone's life.

Either way, mentoring is a pouring of oneself into another person, leveraging your own experiences to help them understand their unique path. Mentoring is a great opportunity to impact someone's life, to strengthen the discipleship ministry in a local congregation, and to further help people to discover the Kingdom life God intends for us.

The author Reggie McNeal suggests some shifts in thinking

that the programmatic church needs to make to accomplish the mission of making disciples of Jesus. The attitudes of the Church take a very long time to change course, just like a large ship at sea, but mentoring relationships can serve as a catalyst for these shifts in attitudes right now. Here's how McNeal describes the needed realignments in his book, *Missional Renaissance:*

- From standardization to customization.
- From scripting to shaping.
- From participation to maturation.
- From delivering to debriefing.
- From didactic to behavioral.
- From curriculum-centered to life-centered.
- From growing into service to growing through service.
- From compartmentalization to integration.
- From age segregation to age integration. [12]

Mentoring enables the discipling of persons by moving from the 'box' of the typical classroom approach to a two-way dynamic of accountability, conversation, and practical life application. Remember, we are seeking to help persons develop the "life ofs" in ways that reflect each person being fully human with their unique quirks and qualifications. Mentoring relationships allow us to accomplish all the things that Reggie McNeal suggests, from customizing the development process, to tailoring the most applicable Kingdom life behaviors, to breaking down the typical age-level barriers inherent in most programmatic approaches. It is a personal approach that keeps people from falling through the cracks or feeling left out.

Who might be a strong mentor?

There are several characteristics that define strong mentors for guiding those in the earlier stages of faith development.

First, these mentors must have a deep faith in Jesus Christ as both Lord and Savior. After all, we are hoping to help people become more like Jesus.

Second, mentors should have a reputation in the faith community for spiritual growth. They will be persons who show strong evidence of moving towards maturity in their development as disciples of Jesus Christ.

Third, they must have a deep commitment to loving God, loving their neighbor, and making disciples of Jesus. These are the three imperatives Jesus gave to us.

Fourth, mentors are most effective when they are blessed by the progress of the mentee rather than any recognition they might receive from the partnership.

Apprenticing

We drew the distinction between apprenticing and mentoring, observing that while mentoring can be broad in scope, apprenticing is usually focused on the transmission of skills.

Phil likes to use the example of his background in radiologic sciences prior to a calling to ministry. As he taught students in the clinical setting at the University of Central Florida, the apprenticing approach was typical. There was, of course, some classroom instruction, but nothing beat the experiential learning of the clinical environment. He would show students how to position the body parts to get the image required, then let them actively assist, and finally the students could take over while an expert monitored their work.

166

A typical understanding of the approach of apprentices is the following formula:

- I do, you watch.
- I do, you help.
- You do, I help.

Dave and Jon Ferguson, in their book, *Exponential,* expand this concept, by adding a component that brings added depth to the process:

- I do. You watch. We talk.
- I do. You help. We talk.
- You do. I help. We talk.
- You do. I watch. We talk.
- You do. Someone else watches. [13]

This expanded approach captures the practice of multiplication, a central theme of their book and of Jesus' life. Disciples are not fully formed disciples if they are not discipling someone else.

We see this very approach in the life and ministry of Jesus. At the beginning of the development of the disciples of Jesus, we find them following Jesus around and observing what he did and how he did it. The disciples are standing off to the side, observing but not yet doing. Often, following a teaching moment or activity, Jesus would take the disciples aside and talk with them about what they had witnessed:

- In Mark 4:1-9, Jesus shares the Parable of the Sower, followed by Mark 4:10-20, where Jesus, alone with the disciples, explains the purpose of the parable and its interpretation.

Jesus does. The disciples watch. They talk.

As the disciples of Jesus begin to develop an emerging under-standing about Jesus' true identity and mission, Jesus invites them to help while he does:

- In Mark 9:14-27, the disciples fail to heal the boy possessed by a spirit, followed by verses 28-29, where Jesus explains that this kind of spirit can only come out by prayer.

The disciples do. Jesus helps. They talk.

As the disciples move toward living fully into their calling, Jesus sends them out on a short-term mission opportunity to put into practice what they have been learning. He gives them the authority, clear instructions, parameters, and expectations for the mission:

- In Matthew 10:5-24, the disciples are sent by Jesus do the things they have witnessed him doing: curing the sick, raising the dead, cleansing the lepers, and casting out demons.

The disciples do. Jesus watches. They talk.

This mentoring/apprenticing approach used by Jesus is still an effective tool for discipleship within a congregation. It is currently most often used by churches to help people develop specific skills:

- **Prayer:** One of the best ways to help someone develop a stronger prayer life is to partner them with a prayer mentor. The mentor is someone known for the depth of their prayer life who commits to a period of time partnering with the mentee to show them how to create a deeper and more impactful prayer life.

In one of the churches Phil served, Margrit, a lady in her 80's, was well known for the deep connection she had with God through prayer — you'll remember her from Phil's earlier story about the time his room key was uncooperative. When someone wanted to grow in the area of prayer, Phil partnered them with Margrit. For many people in that congregation, she became the catalyst for developing a robust prayer life and using this as a pathway to a life opening to God. Every local congregation has people with underappreciated skills that could be utilized to support the development of disciples, if someone asks them to lead in this way.

- **Interpretation/Application of Scripture:** While the typical approach for helping disciples grow in this area of spiritual development is the traditional Bible study, the application of what is being learned to real life scenarios is often a missing component. A mentor can partner with someone to help them learn how to process biblical truths and apply those truths to their individualized life situations.

- **Generosity:** There are many sets of training materials to teach disciples how to handle their finances in a biblical manner. Imagine taking the principles from that training and then pairing a skilled mentor with a struggling partner to develop strong biblical practices and God-given perspectives on the use of financial resources. The combination of instructional principles and real-world experience can make a dramatic difference in implementation.

- **Service:** The best way to help disciples develop a life of service is to partner them with someone who can apprentice them in a particular task or even in leading a service/mission endeavor.

- **Pastoral Care/Compassion:** Many pastors make it a practice to take a member of the congregation with them when they do hospital or home visits. This is a great apprenticing relationship for developing this ministry capacity.

This apprenticing model is also advocated by the Fergusons in their book, *Exponential,* for the multiplication of small groups and small group leaders. They suggest that every small group leader should have at least one apprentice leader that is learning to do what they do in small group leadership/facilitation. This apprentice watches and learns. They have an opportunity to provide leadership under the watchful eye of the leader. When the group has reached a point of needing to multiply, either the leader or apprentice leader can break off with another group member or two to form a new group. Graphically it looks like this.[14]

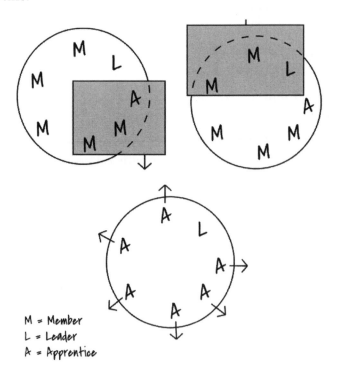

M = Member
L = Leader
A = Apprentice

The apprenticing approach is also a strong tool for the development of leaders for all the ministries of a local congregation. What if, instead of looking through the church phone directory with our Lay Leadership Team and asking who we could get to serve, we were to set up the development of church leaders as an apprenticing process? In this model, every person with a responsibility for any task or area of ministry would be expected to apprentice someone to take over their leadership role in the future.

Who might be the trainer for an apprentice?

The short answer is anyone who is skilled and passionate in an area of ministry and committed to helping someone else become equally proficient in that area:

- Prayer warriors
- Bible scholars
- Bus drivers
- Mission leaders
- Administrative leaders
- Worship leaders
- Sound techs
- Projection techs
- Social media wizards
- Cooks

Imagine the possibilities for a church where everyone with a skill was helping someone else develop that skill!

Coaching

Coaching as a profession is a relatively young career option, but the practice of coaching predates even the time of Jesus. Jesus himself demonstrated coaching skills in the development of his disciples. Coaching, in its purest form, operates from the understanding that the individual being coached already has within them everything they need to be successful. The role of the coach is to draw out those hidden talents and secret strengths, helping individuals find the things they don't know they know about themselves. This is very different from mentoring, in which the role of the mentor is to pour their wisdom, experience, and expertise into the mentee.

In their book on healthy church growth, *Stride,* Mike Schreiner and Ken Willard lay out the attitudes that set coaching apart from other more traditional discipleship strategies:

> Pastor Jim Peich at Morning Star Church likes to refer to the coaching component as the secret sauce in the church's discipleship process.
>
> Imagine a scenario where a person in your current congregation comes to you and says the she really wants to grow as a disciple. You can talk about what she is doing now . . . you listen to her share where she has plugged into the church, and where she is seeing fruit . . . . This is the type of coaching we recommend. It's prayer, discernment, listening, and encouragement. It's suggestions and advice from someone a little further down the path of discipleship. [15]

In a discipleship coaching relationship, the coach partners with the coachee to help them move from where they are to where they want to be in their relationship with God. Chad Hall and Linda Miller, in *Coaching for Christian Leaders,* define this kind of discipleship coaching:

Christian coaching is a focused Christ-centered relationship that cultivates a person's sustained growth and action. [16]

Steve Ogne and Tim Roehl use the word COACH as an acronym to describe the relationship:

C: **C**omes alongside

O: **O**bserves carefully

A: **A**sks questions wisely

C: **C**onsiders options

H: **H**olds accountable [17]

Discipleship coaching is a partnership through which a disciple is able to discern what becoming like Jesus would look like in their life context, understand where they are in relationship to that ideal, explore the possibilities for movement toward that ideal, and develop a plan for accomplishing that goal.

There are many types of partnerships to support personal development. Spiritual development is no exception. The following chart distinguishes between some of them based on who the expert is in each relationship. [18]

The Key Distinction

Who is the expert, using the Me-You index

me ——————————————→ YOU

Consulting
Teaching
Training   *COACHING*
Mentoring
Facilitating
Counseling
Spiritual Direction

©2008 On Purpose Ministry. All rights reserved. Do not duplicate

10

The key distinction in the various partnerships is the idea about who the expert is. In a coaching relationship, the person being coached is the expert. They know their life. They know their goals. They know what they struggle with. They know what they are good at. They are the expert in this relationship. The coach is the expert in the *process* of helping people get clarity and discovering the path forward.

While Jesus did not hang out a shingle as a coach seeking clients for his practice, we do find him practicing amazing coaching skills:

- **Listening:** Jesus practiced listening at levels we can only imagine. He listens to the needs of the disciples, marvels at the lack of understanding in those disciples, hears the pleas of the oppressed, listens to the experiences of those he sent to do the Kingdom work, and hears the heart — not just the spoken words — of those seeking him:

    Everyone should be quick to listen, slow to speak.
    James 1:19

- **Encouraging/Acknowledging:** The Gospels are replete with examples of Jesus encouraging the disciples. Encouragement or acknowledgement is a way of affirming progress in understanding or life application. Genuine encouragement should reflect these qualities:

    ○ It should be authentic.

    ○ It should be unequivocal — no "maybes."

    ○ It should be enthusiastic.

    ○ It should be specific.

    ○ It should be substantive — reflecting not just "what" but "who" the recipient is.

Consider, for example, the response of Jesus as the seventy-two return from their mission (as related in Luke 10):

> **The seventy-two returned with joy and said, "Lord, even the demons submit to us in your name." He replied, "I saw Satan fall like lightning from heaven. I have given you authority to trample on snakes and scorpions and to overcome all the power of the enemy."**
>
> **Luke 10:17-19**

Or Jesus' response to Simon Peter when Peter demonstrated his understanding of the role of Jesus:

> **"Blessed are you, Simon son of Jonah, for this was not revealed to you by flesh and blood but by my Father in heaven."**
>
> **Matthew 16:17**

- **Asking Powerful Questions:** One of the most powerful tools in the coaching toolkit is the asking of powerful questions. These are questions that invite the person being coached to dig deeper, discover motivations, and explore possibilities. Jesus was the master of powerful questioning. It was a tool he used often, with over 200 questions posed by Jesus recorded in the Gospels:

  - Who do you say that I am?

  - Do you want to get well?

  - Do you also want to leave?

  - What profit would there be for one to gain the whole world and forfeit his life?

  - What do you wish?

The power of questions is that they get us to persuade ourselves, which is always a better way for people to see their way forward than being told what to do.

- **Responding Appropriately:** There are a variety of methods of response to choose from when engaging with a disciple seeking the way forward in the Kingdom life, from paraphrasing, to truth-telling, to giving advice. Jesus used them all. When the Pharisees question the disciples about Jesus eating with sinners, Jesus responds:

> "It is not the healthy who need a doctor, but the sick. I have not come to call the righteous but sinners."
>
> **Mark 2:17**

That's an excellent example of prophetic truth-telling. He could pivot seamlessly to an excellent use of metaphor using everyday objects to give inspirational direction:

> He said to them, "Do you bring in a lamp to put it under a bowl or a bed? Instead, don't you put it on its stand? For whatever is hidden is meant to be disclosed, and whatever is concealed is meant to be brought out into the open."
>
> **Mark 4:21-22**

- **Negotiating Actions:** Coaching is action-oriented and future-focused. As a wise mentor once said, "Without action there is no coaching." Jesus modeled this dynamic approach as he constantly encouraged his disciples to understand something, go somewhere, say something, share something, or serve someone. Listen to the negotiated action of the demoniac as the demons leave him:

The man from whom the demons had gone begged that he might be with him; but Jesus sent him away, saying, "Return to your home, and declare how much God has done for you." So he went away, proclaiming throughout the city how much Jesus had done for him.

Luke 8:38-39

We have previously discussed characteristics that anchor a good discipling relationship. Coaching as a discipling technique creates an amenable atmosphere for these qualities to flourish:

- **It's Relational:** By its very definition, coaching is relational. It's a partnership. The efficacy of the coaching process is based on the trust developed in a relationship. It is the relationship that creates a 'safe space' for deeper reflection, greater understanding, and creative approaches to continuing development. That relationship is based on the coach being an advocate and trusted confidant.

- **It's Focused:** The coaching process is developed around a focused outcome identified by the disciple. The disciple sets the agenda, identifies the focus of the conversations, and explores the possibilities for the future.

- **It's Intentional:** One of the big 'wins' of a coaching relationship is the intentionality of the process. There is an expressed goal, followed by an exploration of the possibilities for reaching the goal, the building of a plan for accomplishing the goal, and support in attaining the goal.

- **It's Developmental:** While an individual coaching session may be focused on resolving a specific issue, a larger outcome of the process is the development of a disciple's ability to deal with similar issues in the future. Coaching is not just about fixing something. It is about developing the person to be their own confident fixer.

177

- **It's Accountable:** The coach serves as an accountability partner for the disciple in the sense of the disciple being held accountable to themselves. Greater progress is made when there is a sense of accountability — when the disciple knows that someone will ask about their progress.

Discipleship coaching, in the context of a local congregation, can take a couple of different forms. Most congregations have some form of small group gathering. Typically, these gatherings include some facilitated learning experience as well as pastoral care and prayer. The research is clear that while these small group gatherings are great for fellowship and the dissemination of information, the impact in terms of transformation is limited. However, introducing a coaching component into the typical small group Bible study can literally lead to transformed lives. Don Everts, Doug Schaupp, and Val Gordon, in *Breaking the Huddle,* describe how introducing the 'response' element into the discipleship cycle can dramatically change the impact. They call it a "putting-it-into-action" group. The group leader sets the stage this way:

> For the next few months, let's get together weekly to discuss fairly straightforward passages from the four Gospels and then brainstorm specific action steps that we will actually commit to doing. The following week each of us will share what we tried, what happened, and what we saw God do.

> It was clear: "Let's decide what we want to do." They left very clear about what they were committing to do in the coming week. [19]

Notice the focus, relationships, intentionality, development, and accountability in this simple change to a small group ministry setting.

Discipleship coaching offers a strong alternative to the typical programmatic approach of classes, short-term small group studies, and the one-size-fits-all brand of educational support offered in most local congregations. It focuses instead on the needs and development of the individual disciple, wherever they are along the pathway to becoming like Jesus. Discipleship coaching can be a one-to-one partnership or a small group collaboration (triads recommended). Discipleship coaches practice the same skills demonstrated by Jesus.

The focus of a discipleship coaching session is determined by the disciple being coached. The role of the coach is to guide the process of discovery and development. The following coaching conversation model is a simple tool showing the desired flow of a coaching conversation.[20]

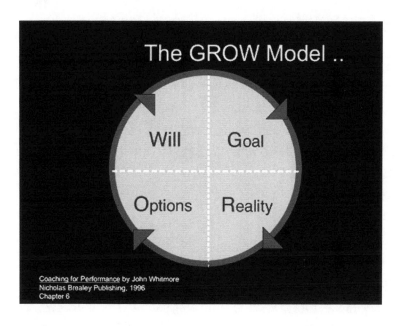

The GROW Model ..

Will   Goal

Options   Reality

Coaching for Performance by John Whitmore
Nicholas Brealey Publishing, 1996
Chapter 6

People who make great coaches share these attributes:

- **They are spiritually mature:** They have a reputation for strong faith, growing as a disciple, and regularly practicing the disciplines of the spiritual life.

- **They are selfless:** They find joy in helping others be successful — the coach rarely gets the spotlight!

- **They are relational:** They understand that the key to coaching is the relationship. The coach needs to like people.

- **They are self-aware:** The coach must know his/her strengths/weaknesses, baggage, and behavioral preferences.

- **They are enthusiastic advocates:** They believe in the person being coached.

- **They are action-oriented:** Without action, there is no coaching.

There are a variety of tools for supporting the discipleship coaching process. A widely used resource in United Methodist circles is the Real Discipleship Survey; we have highlighted snippets of it in several chapters (available at emc3coaching. com). This tool is a self-identifying discipleship resource helping the disciple ascertain where they are on a continuum toward maturity in the six dimensions of discipleship presented previously. It is designed to be a conversation-starter for a discipling relationship.

For congregations interested in training discipleship coaches, the *Coaching for Discipleship* (available at www. emc3coaching.com) may be a helpful resource.

For more information on this approach to small groups, see the *Small Group Leader Training Guide,* available through www.emc3coaching.com.

Additional Resources You May Find Helpful

- Linda J. Miller and Chad W. Hall, *Coaching for Christian Leaders*

- Chad Hall, Bill Copper, and Kathryn McElveen, *Faith Coaching*

Questions for Reflection and Discussion

1. Descriptions were presented of several discipleship roles and/or skills. Which of these seems to come most naturally to you? How have you employed these skills or functioned in these roles?

2. In what ways is life as a disciple becoming like Jesus modeled in your congregation? How does this impact the life and ministry of the church?

3. Compare your own experiences with small groups to the way Jesus ran his small group ministry? What similarities and differences do you see?

4. Distinguish between the type of teaching done by Jesus and the approach often used in the programmatic ministries in the Church.

5. One of the ways Jesus developed disciples was to pour himself into them (mentor them). Why might someone be drawn to you as a mentor for their journey?

6. What skill or ability do you have that would be helpful to pass along in an apprenticing relationship?

Conclusion

The vision that Jesus cast for our world, couched in the language of the "Kingdom of God" or "Kingdom of Heaven" is nothing short of amazing. Jesus invites us to share a vision of a world happening right now, where we are engaged in an intimate relationship with the One who created us, living in ways that bring honor and glory to that Creator, taking part in authentic relationships with other people, sharing our resources so that no one is in need, and defining our lives in terms of the difference we can make rather than what we can get.

The early Church provided a glimpse of what this could look like in Acts 2:

> **They devoted themselves to the apostles' teaching and to fellowship, to the breaking of bread and to prayer. Everyone was filled with awe at the many wonders and signs performed by the apostles. All the believers were together and had everything in common. They sold property and possessions to give to anyone who had need. Every day they continued to meet together in the temple courts. They broke bread in their homes and ate together with glad and sincere hearts, praising God and enjoying the favor of all the people. And the Lord added to their number daily those who were being saved.**
>
> **Acts 2:42-47**

It is the kind of life that God intended for us. And though it seems in many ways like a shining, unattainable dream, it is possible. Jesus showed us how to do it. The early Church also modeled this new way of living. But, this kind of life doesn't happen by wishful thinking. It takes a clear vision, focus, intentionality, and accountability.

That is what discipleship is all about.

The dynamic model of the Acts 2 church feels, in many ways, like ancient history. In contemporary practice, the responsibility for making disciples has been shifted from relational accountability to programmatic ministries. Jesus showed us a better way — not only for living but for making disciples. He cast a clear vision with two parts:

> **"Love the Lord your God with all your heart, all your soul, all your mind, and all your strength and love your neighbor as yourself."**
>
> **Luke 22:37**

> **"Go, therefore, and make disciples of all nations. . . ."**
>
> **Matthew 28:19, NIV**

Every disciple has the responsibility for both imperatives.

We hope this resource has reminded you about the call for all who say they will follow him to make Jesus' vision a reality. None of the strategies we have discussed here require big facilities, large gatherings, professional staff, or big budgets. They do require a longing to discover the abundant Kingdom life that God intends and a heart for helping others do the same.

There is no 'set' way to live into any of these imperatives.

Each person is unique, and what is helpful for one may be an obstacle for another. This is true for both our personal development and for the ways that we are called to support others in the journey.

We hope this book has provided insights and tools that will make your progress smoother. We, at Excellence in Ministry Coaching have many other resources to help you and your church on your way — let us know how we can help.

How will you live more fully into becoming more like Jesus and make disciples like Jesus did? It's up to you.

God bless you and grant you courage as you grow and lead others.

Phil and Eddie, April 2020

Works Cited

Chapter One: Defining Discipleship

1. As shared in a TED talk by Anne Curzon at ideas.ted.com.

2. Dennis McCallum and Jessica Lowery, *Organic Discipleship,* New Paradigm Press, 2012, p. 2.

3. https://en.wikipedia.org/wiki/Disciple_(Christianity).

4. Dan Dick, "Disciple Dissipation," Insight, April 2012.

5. Dallas Willard, *The Spirit of the Disciplines: Understanding How God Changes Lives,* HarperCollins Publishing, 1998.

6. N.T. Wright, *After You Believe,* HarperCollins Publishers, 2010, p. 111.

7. Ibid, p. 107.

8. Ibid, p. 118.

9. Ibid, p. 124.

Chapter Two: What Discipleship Looks Like

1. Alan Hirsch, *The Forgotten Ways,* Brazos Press, 2016, p. 122.

2. Dallas Willard, *The Great Omission,* HarperCollins, 2006, p. 65.

3. www.forbes.com/sites/taraswart/2018/03/27/the-4-underlying-principles-to-changing-your-brain/#7d676cae5a71.

4. George Barna, *Maximum Faith: Live Like Jesus,* Metaformation Inc., Strategenius Group, and WHC Publishing, 2011, p. 35.

5. Adapted from the work of Rev. Dr. Steve Manskar, *Forming Christian Disciples,* published by Discipleship Resources, Nashville, TN.

6. www.housechurch.org/miscellaneous/wesley_band-societies.html.

7. James White, *Rethinking the Church,* Baker Press, 2003, pp. 76-77.

8. Barna, *Maximum Faith,* pp. 8-9.

9. Louis Giglio, "The Air I Breathe," *Wired for a life of Worship: Student edition,* Multnomah Books, 2006, p. 48.

10. Brother Lawrence, *The Practice of the Presence of God,* Spire Books, 1958, pp. 11-12.

11. Henri Nouwen, as quoted by Eric Cooter, "21st Century Wells: Christian Community in the Third Place," *Ministry Matters,* March 11, 2013, www.ministrymatters.com.

12. Eugene Peterson, *Eat This Book,* Eerdmans Publishing Company, 2006, p. 15.

13. www.passiton.com/inspirational-quotes/7155-do-all-the-good-you-can-by-all-the-means-you.

14. www.resourceumc.org/en/content/john-wesley-on-giving.

Chapter Three: Belonging to the Body of Christ

1. Phil Maynard, *Shift 2.0,* Market Square Books, 2018.

2. Ken Gire, *The Reflective Life: Becoming More Spiritually Sensitive to the Everyday Moments of Life,* Chariot Victor Publishing, 1998.

3. Henri Nouwen, as quoted by Eric Cooter, "21st Century Wells: Christian Community in the Third Place," *Ministry Matters,* March 11, 2013, www.ministrymatters.com.

4. Michael Frost, *Surprise the World,* NavPress, 2016, pp. 7-8.

5. Janice Price as quoted by Michael Frost, *Surprise the World,* p. 43.

6. Albert L. Winseman, *Growing an Engaged Church,* The Gallup Organization, 2006, p. 103.

7. Alan Hirsch, *The Forgotten Ways,* Brazos Press, 2006, pp. 133-134.

8. Ibid.

9. Alan Hirsch and Lance Ford, *Right Here, Right Now,* Baker Books, 2011, p. 203.

10. Jim Ozier and Fiona Hayworth, *Clip-In: Risking Hospitality in Your Church,* Abingdon Press, 2014, pp. 133-134.

Chapter Four: Becoming More Like Jesus

1. Dallas Willard, *The Spirit of the Disciplines,* HarperCollins Publishing, p. 158.

2. Adapted from the work of Rev. Dr. Steve Manskar, *Forming Christian Disciples,* published by Discipleship Resources, Nashville, TN.

3. Dallas Willard, *The Spirit of the Disciplines*, p. 147.

4. Greg Ogden, *Transforming Discipleship*, IVP Books, 2003, p. 34.

5. Barna, *Maximum Faith*, pp. 6-7.

Chapter Five: Blessing the World

1. Eric Rees, *S.H.A.P.E.* (adapted), Zondervan Publishing, 2006.

2. www.ImagineGenerosity.com.

3. Michael Slaughter, *Change the World,* Abingdom Press, 2010, p. 63.

Chapter Six: Growing Disciples

1. *The Book of Discipline of The United Methodist Church,* United Methodist Publishing House, 2012.

2. George Barna, *Growing True Disciples,* WaterBrook, 2001.

3. Adapted from Greg L. Hawkins & Cally Parkinson, Move: *What 1,000 Churches Reveal About Spiritual Growth,* Willow Creek Association, 2011.

4. Stephen Covey, *The 7 Habits of Highly Effective People,* Simon and Schuster Publishing, 1989, p. 97.

5. Michael Hyatt, "The Leadership Strategy of Jesus," michaelhyatt.com, March 24, 2010.

6. Greg Ogden, *Transforming Discipleship,* p. 145.

7. www.churchleadership.com/leading-ideas/are-you-teaching-people-about-faith-or-how-to-practice-it/?id=li20200311.

Chapter Seven: Discipling Relationships and Skills

1. www.goodreads.com/quotes/22155-i-like-your-christ-i-do-not-like-your-christians.

2. David Kinnamon and Gabe Lyons, *UnChristian,* Baker Books, 2007.

3. Adapted from Greg L. Hawkins & Cally Parkinson, Move: *What 1,000 Churches Reveal About Spiritual Growth,* Willow Creek Association, 2011.

4. www.forbes.com/sites/kevinkruse/2013/04/09/what-is-leader-ship/#79dd5dae5b90.

5. www.britannica.com/science/observational-learning.

6. Dave Ferguson and Warren Bird, in *Hero Maker: Five Essential Practices for Leaders to Multiply Leaders,* Zondervan, 2018.

7. Suzanne Goebel, *Coaching Foundations Training,* On-Purpose Ministry, 2002.

8. Rebert E. Logan and Charles R. Ridley, *The Discipleship Difference,* Logan Leadership Publishing, 2015, p. 100.

9. www.leadershipfreak.blog/2014/08/22/take-mentoring-to-the-next-level/.

10. www.sundayschoolrevolutionary.com/mentoring-apprentic-ing-and-coaching-for-revolutionary-sunday-school/.

11. Val Hastings, *Accelerated Coach Training,* Coaching 4 Clergy, 2011, p. 6.

12. Reggie McNeal, *Missional Renaissance,* Jossey-Bass Publishing, 2009, pp. 95-109.

13. Dave and Jon Ferguson, *Exponential,* Zondervan Publishing, 2010, p. 63.

14. Ibid, pp. 96-97.

15. Mike Schreiner and Ken Willard, *Stride,* Abingdon Press, 2017, pp. 66-67.

16. Linda J. Miller and Chad W. Hall, *Coaching for Christian Leaders,* Chalice Press, 2007, p. 10.

17. Steve Ogne and Tim Roehl, *Transformissional Coaching,* B & H Publishing Group, 2008.

18. Suzanne Goebel, "Key Distinctions" graphic, *Coaching Foundations Training,* On Purpose Ministry, 2002.

19. Everts, Schaupp, and Gordon, *Breaking the Huddle,* IVP Books, 2016, p. 104.

20. John Whitmore, *Coaching for Performance,* Nicholas Brealey Publishing, 1986, Chapter 6.

NEXT GENERATION
SMALL GROUPS
Complete Kits for Virtual Groups

These resources are based on current books published by Market Square, and each package will include:

- A live, online, "Lead the Leader" session with book authors, to demonstrate the use of their books with small groups.

- Digital copies of the book, for distribution to members of the small group.

- A detailed Leader's Guide, which can be used by a group facilitator to walk the group through the session.

- A PowerPoint slideshow which can be used with each weekly session to assist the leader/facilitator in moving the group through the session.

- Participant handouts, which can be sent to each group member before each weekly meeting.

Our first two studies, both eight-week sessions, are now available at:

nextgensmallgroups.com

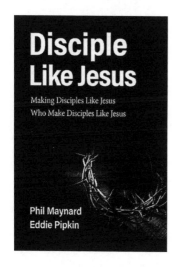

Other Titles
from Market Square Books
marketsquarebooks.com

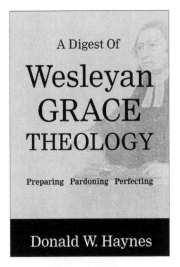

Wesleyan Grace Theology

Dr. Donald Haynes

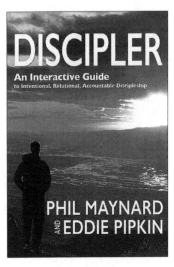

Discipler

Phil Maynard & Eddie Pipkin

Strategy Matters

Your Roadmap for an Effective Ministry Planning Retreat

Kay Kotan & Ken Willard

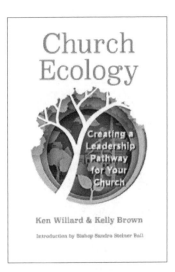

Church Ecology

Ken Willard & Kelly Brown

Grow Your Church

with these books from Market Square

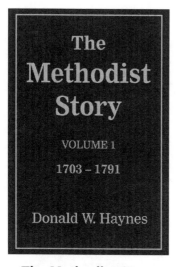

The Methodist Story
Volume I · 1703-1791

Dr. Donald Haynes

Shift 2.0

Dr. Phil Maynard

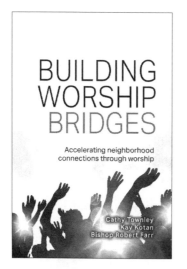

Building Worship Bridges

Cathy Townley

Get Out of That Box!

Anne Bosarge

Latest Titles
from Market Square Books
marketsquarebooks.com

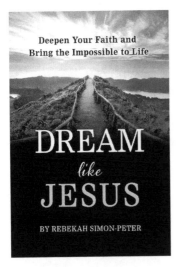

Dream Like Jesus
Bring the Impossible to Life
Rebekah Simon-Peter

From Franchise
To Local Dive
Jason Moore & Rosario Picardo

The Methodist Story
Volume 2 ▪ 1792-2019
Dr. Donald W. Haynes

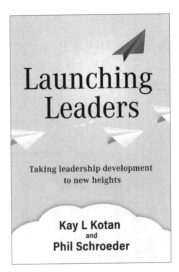

Launching Leaders
Leadership Development
Kay Kotan and Phil Schroeder

NEXT GENERATION
SMALL GROUPS
Complete Kits for Virtual Groups

Everything needed for a 6-week small group study of *Disciple Like Jesus*
(except the members)

A virtual study kit from Next Generation Small Groups includes everything needed for a 6-week study of *Disciple Like Jesus*. These virtual kits are perfect for groups that meet online or in a traditional setting.

- A live, online, "Lead the Leader" session with Dr. Phil Maynard, to demonstrate the use of *Disciple Like Jesus* with small groups.

- Digital copies of *Disciple Like Jesus*, for distribution to each member of the group.

- A detailed Leader's Guide, which can be used by your group facilitator to walk the members through each session.

- A PowerPoint slideshow which can be used with each weekly session to assist the facilitator in moving the group through the session.

- Participant handouts, which can be sent to group members before each weekly meeting.

nextgensmallgroups.com